CU00903966

MULTI-LEVEL
MARKETING

MULTI-LEVEL MARKETING

A PRACTICAL GUIDE TO SUCCESSFUL NETWORK SELLING

PETER J CLOTHIER

KOGAN
PAGE

For Debbie

First published in 1990

Apart from any fair dealing for the purposes of research or private study, or criticism or review, as permitted under the Copyright, Designs and Patents Act, 1988, this publication may only be reproduced, stored or transmitted, in any form or by any means, with the prior permission in writing of the publishers, or in the case of reprographic reproduction in accordance with the terms of licences issued by the Copyright Licensing Agency. Enquiries concerning reproduction outside those terms should be sent to the publishers at the undermentioned address:

Kogan Page Ltd,
120 Pentonville Road
London N1 9JN

© Peter J Clothier, 1990

British Library Cataloguing in Publication Data

A CIP record for this book is available from the British Library.

ISBN 0-7494-0079-X
       0-7494-0087-0 Pbk

Typeset by DP Photosetting, Aylesbury, Bucks
Printed and bound in Great Britain by
Biddles Ltd, Guildford and Kings Lynn

Contents

Acknowledgements

Many people have assisted with the production of this book in various ways – thanks are due to all of them. In particular I would like to extend my appreciation to:

Paul for planting the seed;

all the companies who responded to my requests for information;

Richard Berry for background information and other assistance;

the company representatives and distributors who gave up their valuable time to be interviewed;

Debbie, Erica and Philippa for their patience, understanding and encouragement.

Preface

Many of the best books on all types of subject have been written, not by the most successful practitioners in those subjects, or by those continually engrossed in those subjects, but by people with the desire and ability to thoroughly research and write about the subject from an unbiased and objective viewpoint.

I have been a Trading Standards Officer for fifteen years. It is a profession which can develop a healthy cynicism in anybody, and I am no exception – since careful and honest traders cause few complaints, one hears mainly about the rogues, the careless and the incompetent. And my cynicism should be even more pronounced because I have been dealing specifically with investigations into consumer frauds, including bogus business opportunities, for six years.

Imagine my reaction when my USA-based brother visited me in England and told me about the wonderful business opportunity offered by a company he had stumbled upon. He suggested I should participate without delay. Out came the stock comments, especially, 'It'll saturate – I can prove it!', but after my brother went home I thought more about the concept I had seen; it fascinated and intrigued me. I made enquiries, read about it, researched it thoroughly. I met the people in the business, I went to the meetings and rallies, I learned everything I could about the business – how it worked and how to make it work – and I am still learning. I have interviewed very successful distributors and several large MLM companies. I have seen, heard and experienced the positive and the negative sides of MLM, so I believe I can give you full, unbiased and factual information concerning almost everything you will need (and want) to know about the business and how to make it work for you.

Introduction

This is the first comprehensive and widely available book ever written in the UK on what is probably the best opportunity of the 1990s, for a person without experience or capital, to build a highly profitable business of their own without taking any significant risks. This successful and increasingly popular method of distributing goods and services has brought wealth to people who never thought it would be possible for them. It has also doubled, tripled and sometimes quadrupled the income of people who thought that they were doing pretty well already.

It is a mystery why such a tremendous business concept has lain virtually hidden from the general public for so long; indeed, it has not even been properly recognized within the business world for the potentially lucrative marketing concept that it is. I challenge you to find *one* book, out of the thousands available on the subject of starting a business or working full-time or part-time from home, which explains the concept and potential of a genuine multi-level marketing opportunity for the benefit of its readers. There are a handful of American books on the subject (the concept is well developed over there), including a few written about specific companies, but these are not to be found on the shelves of your local bookshop at a reasonable price. Some UK books examine franchising, party-plan selling and door-to-door sales, but that is as near to multi-level marketing (or MLM) as they come. Anyone who knows, *really* knows, anything about the concept will be aware of how much more there is to MLM. Most books will do no more than give a warning about the perils of being lured into a 'pyramid scheme'. Here you will read how the multi-level distribution concept (like any other form of business method) can be abused and perverted into an illegal and immoral con-trick. You will also learn how to identify the wrong schemes and steer well clear of them.

So, there is a need for a book on this subject. It is not right that a business so simple yet so full of potential continues to remain a mystery for thousands of people who may be looking for the right opportunity.

What exactly *is* multi-level marketing, or, as it is also known, 'network marketing'? The answer to this question will be examined in detail in the following chapters but, simply put, it is one of many methods of moving products from the manufacturer to the retail customer. The basic principle of MLM, however, is that the complete sales force is developed by the salespeople themselves. Those putting the greatest efforts into this activity reach the highest 'levels' and consequently receive the greatest rewards.

MLM has developed in the UK over three decades, and is now a substantial method of doing business. The Direct Selling Association's 1989 survey reports that in 1988 MLM accounted for sales worth more than £87,000,000, approximately 15 per cent of all direct sales (sales direct to private individuals at home and at work, initiated and concluded by a salesperson). At the end of 1988 around 168,000 people in the UK were part-time or full-time MLM distributors, an increase of 29 per cent over twelve months. These facts, when considered with the growth in all forms of directly-sold products and services (currently around 12 per cent per year, to over £577,000,000 in 1988), show how important MLM is within the UK economy as a method of doing business. In the USA the concept has been developed to a far greater extent over many decades, to the point where almost any goods or services can be obtained through MLM. It is a multi-national, multi-million-pound business involving millions of people.

MLM is a legal, ethical, successful, ever-expanding business method with which anyone can make as much or as little extra income as they wish, with no financial risk, in six or sixty hours a week, so why the secrecy about it? Why is there no factual unbiased guide to starting and developing a MLM business generally available? I suspect the answer may be summed up in the two words 'pyramid selling', a phrase which arouses suspicion and causes confusion in the uninformed, but which is more correctly used to describe a rash of highly undesirable abuses of the multi-level concept in the early 1970s. At that time many people were left disillusioned, dejected and considerably out of pocket. The methods which caused such a public outcry were swiftly outlawed and have rarely been seen since, but the bad taste left in many mouths lingers.

I hope this book will help to redress the balance and put MLM where it belongs – in the public eye as a respectable and successful business method offering an excellent business opportunity of vast potential to all kinds of people. It is intended to complement the hundreds of books currently available dealing with all other kinds of business opportunities. It is a factual and helpful guide to:

- anyone looking for a risk-free business which can be built to whatever size is desired;
- anyone who has been introduced to and is considering joining a particular multi-level marketing scheme and who is unsure about any aspect of it;
- anyone called upon to advise enquirers on such matters;
- current MLM distributors wishing to broaden their knowledge of the business generally;
- students of sales and marketing methods;
- dubious and suspicious friends and relatives of multi-level distributors.

In the following chapters you will find:

- a full description of the MLM concept, including details of how sales networks are developed, how payments and commissions are calculated and how MLM resembles and differs from conventional businesses;
- what the special benefits of MLM are, and why you cannot fail;
- interviews with some of the most successful distributors in the UK;
- help in making a decision whether to participate and which company to join;
- key advice on developing your MLM business;
- answers to all the common criticisms and misunderstandings about the business method;
- how to conduct your business legally and ethically;
- a list of many of the companies offering a MLM business in the UK;
- where to get (even more) information.

A request

This is a fairly comprehensive book, but there are bound to be a few aspects that I have not covered, and maybe even some errors. I would be grateful to be informed of any such matters for future editions. Readers' success stories (especially if inspired by this book!) are welcomed for possible future inclusion.

1: What is Multi-level Marketing?

This chapter will:

- show you what *you* can achieve with multi-level marketing;
- introduce you to the concept of MLM;
- tell you about the past, the present and the future of MLM.

What can MLM do for you?

More accurately, what can *you* do with MLM? There are over 500,000 millionaires in the USA today and at least 20 per cent of them achieved this through MLM in the last 10 years. This may give you some idea of the wealth-creating potential of MLM. You may have no desire to become rich, but do read on. You have almost certainly started reading this book because of a desire to increase your income to some extent. You may come to the conclusion after reading this book that MLM is not for you; that's fine – it doesn't appeal to everyone. However, MLM allows you to create any amount of extra income that you wish to have. You can fit it around your current lifestyle and commitments in any way you choose, or you can go into it full-time from the start. You can work part-time in MLM until your income from it exceeds your current income, enabling you to give up full-time employment. You can use it to produce some extra pocket money each week or you can decide to become a millionaire within a few years.

Most people realize at some stage in their life that wealth is rarely obtained by working for somebody else. Working for yourself is not a guarantee of future wealth but it is almost certainly the only way that you will have a chance of making a great deal of money. Once you are in full-time employment, however, you need some nerve to cut off a steady and reliable salary in order to take the necessary risks involved in starting your own business. But are those risks really 'necessary'? With MLM the answer is *no*! It is not necessary to resign from a full-time job to start in MLM, neither is it necessary to take financial risks of any significance.

You may say, 'Sounds great, but I've never been in business in my life. Who's going to help me get started and tell me what I need to do?' How about unlimited help and advice from people already successful in the business?

What's the catch?

It all sounds too good to be true; there must be a catch somewhere. No catch. Can any business be so flexible and yet have such vast potential? Yes, MLM is infinitely flexible and virtually unlimited in potential. What experience and qualifications are necessary to start, or succeed, in MLM? No experience or qualifications are necessary. Your background, financial position, education and social class are irrelevant. MLM is a great economic leveller – earnings are in direct proportion to effort. (In Chapter 8 you will read how people from entirely different backgrounds have become very wealthy in MLM.) The only entry requirement is the payment of a joining fee (maximum £75 at present, set by law). The only requirements for success are a strong desire for the level of success you want and a willingness to learn how to attain it. For further details on these points see later chapters.

So far only MLM's financial potential has been discussed. That's not all it offers. Indeed, many successful distributors see the other benefits of the business as being of equal importance as the money they make from it. Friendships are made, there is personal development and the opportunity to help people. These and other aspects are explored in more depth later.

Is it legal?

Not many types of business method have their own specific legislation to ensure fair play. As long as these are complied with (in addition to other general trading laws), then MLM is perfectly legal.

A number of the most reputable direct selling companies formed the Direct Selling Association in 1965. A code of practice was drawn up and approved by the Office of Fair Trading; this governs all aspects of DSA members' activities. The code ensures ethical practices by all members, a number of which use the MLM distribution method.

How does it work?

How are these large earnings possible? First, let's look at other types of income.

Linear income This is familiar to everyone; you work for a month, you get paid for a month's work, you work another month . . . or perhaps you knit a jumper, you get paid for that jumper, you knit another jumper, and so on. Even though certain professions offer the opportunity to earn incredibly large linear incomes, they are in almost all cases limited to certain levels and require a daily commitment. Often a *very* long day is demanded.

Residual income This is income earned in respect of work done at some time in the past which remains economically relevant for a certain period of time. The obvious example is a music artiste whose recordings continue to sell for long periods after being made. Residual earnings are a prime source of income in the world of insurance, as policies sold in previous years continue to be renewed. The commission on these amounts is added to the current year's earnings and can create substantial annual earnings. Actors and authors earn residual income as long as their films continue to be shown and their books read. It is possible in this way that a small number of highly successful records, films or books can provide a lifetime's income for the creator.

'Multiplex' income MLM takes advantage of what has been termed 'multiplex' income. This is a form of residual income, as it provides current earnings based on past efforts. In addition, however, income is provided in respect of the efforts of others. This is no different from the way many major corporations earn their income from a large network of independent distributors or franchises, except that in MLM the necessary advertising budget is only a fraction of that spent in other types of business. If multiplex

income sounds like some kind of unfair exploitation, bear in mind that *every* distributor in the organization has the opportunity to take advantage of it. Even though other people's efforts can benefit you, remember also that those others are only there because of your past efforts in sponsoring them (or sponsoring the person who sponsored them, and so on).

Quite simply, MLM is one of many ways of selling goods and services. There is (or should be) no mystique about the method. It is a successful and straightforward marketing concept which can be applied to virtually any consumer product or service. It is as legitimate and ethical a business as any other, if not more so, as you will see further on in the book. It is very big business, and getting bigger all the time. The basic principles of MLM which make it so different from conventional methods of product distribution are:

- how the sales force is constructed;
- how the profits are shared;
- how the products are sold.

Let's look at a 'normal' business; the paint industry, for example. The manufacturer needs to sell his production in the largest quantities possible, to maximize profit. He needs to employ salespeople to obtain orders from large wholesalers. On top of the cost of production of the paint will be added salary costs, distribution costs, advertising costs, other overheads and some profit element. There are now perhaps twenty wholesalers who need to sell as much of the paint as possible to retail outlets. The wholesaler now has to add to the cost of each can of paint the cost of his staff, his premises, advertising and other essentials, plus some profit, and supplies perhaps a hundred retailers with paint. Each retailer adds his mark-up to the product to cover staff, administration, premises, collection, delivery and profit, and hopes to have, say, five hundred customers. Each trader has had to invest a large amount of money in premises, equipment and stock, and probably the greatest motivator for each of them is negative fear of bankruptcy or something similar.

It requires only very simple mathematics to calculate that the paint manufacturer now relies upon a network of two thousand distributors supplying fifty thousand retail customers. The manufacturer and each distributor take a percentage of the retail price for themselves, and if they can find more traders or consumers to supply to they can increase profitability. The larger each distributor's order from his supplier, the larger the discount he can negotiate. Now visualize the network as described in the form of circles and lines of supply. It can be converted into a multi-level distribution network by doing nothing at all.

A multi-level distribution network looks essentially the same. This fact is crucial to understanding that MLM is a straightforward marketing concept. The structure of an MLM network is no different in principle from any other system of distributing goods. Each person in the network buys goods at a price dependent upon the amount purchased and receives a percentage of the retail price as profit.

So where *does* MLM differ from conventional businesses?

The sales force

The most obvious difference is that the wholesalers and retailers in the above-mentioned network are replaced by distributors. Each distributor may supply other distributors, supply consumers, or supply himself. The paint manufacturer looks for existing wholesalers to whom he can sell his product, and likewise the wholesalers will supply existing retailers. In MLM *every* distributor has been personally introduced to the business by the manufacturer or, more likely, by an existing distributor. In the conventional business the salespersons are usually employed staff. In MLM the distributors are the salespersons, and they are self-employed.

When a new MLM company wishes to introduce a product into the market place it will firstly choose a nucleus of enthusiastic people in key areas across the country and teach them everything about the product and the marketing plan to be used (every one is different and various types will be examined later). The company will then assist these original distributors to sponsor (recruit) further distributors, and so on, by putting on seminars and other business opportunity meetings around the country. The rate of growth of the company's sales depends entirely on the commitment of their distributor force in selling the product and sponsoring more distributors.

Profit sharing

Who gets a share of the profits in the normal business world? The recipients will be the owners and directors of the various distribution businesses, and maybe the travelling salesmen employed by the manufacturer and wholesaler. Very rarely will the retailer's sales staff share the profits, however excellent and hardworking they may be. They will probably earn exactly the same as their colleagues who avoid work whenever possible and whose attitude loses the firm many customers.

In any case, how much profit is there to be shared in a normal company? A large proportion of the profit will be spent on advertising, salaries, premises, stockholding, administration, and a hundred other costs. The marketing of a new product can cost millions of pounds in advertising and promotion.

In contrast, an MLM company's costs on these items will be only a small fraction of a normal company's outlay. Virtually no advertising is used, except that directed to the distributors themselves. Salary costs do not include salespersons as none are employed, and administration is therefore far less. These savings, plus, of course, the company's profit on the sales of goods to its distributors, enable a central fund to be created. From this fund special bonuses may be paid to distributors, based on the sales performance of the organizations developed by each of them. In this way every distributor is paid in direct proportion to his or her efforts.

The MLM company's savings may also allow them to spend more on research and development; consequently the products involved are usually of excellent quality.

Selling the products

Virtually all MLM sales are made by 'direct selling'. This is defined by the Direct Selling Association as follows:

'The selling of consumer goods direct to private individuals, in their homes and places of work, through transactions initiated and concluded by the salesperson.'

It is obviously different from the way most consumer goods are sold, through shops, catalogues and direct mail. Direct selling is, of course, not exclusive to MLM products, and anyone will be aware of the many types of goods sold 'direct' by party-plan, person-to-person and door-to-door.

Direct selling has certain advantages over shop retailing, for the customer, the salesperson and the manufacturer. The customer doesn't have to leave home and the products are delivered. This has great appeal to old or frail people, and it also appeals to busy people who would rather avoid battling through town-centre shops. Many goods sold through MLM and other direct selling methods are unique in some way, and would be hard to find in a retail shop. The customer is likely to receive a great deal more personal attention from the salesperson than he can expect at a shop. With person-to-person sales, the seller has an opportunity of developing a friendly relationship with the customer, if the latter is not already a friend. This relationship is vital for repeat sales to the customer, and also allows new products to be introduced and demonstrated on a regular basis. This distributor/customer relationship is also important to the company; it takes the place of the national advertising which a conventional company would need to attract its customers to the retail outlets.

Past, present and future

The basic concept of MLM is far too simple and attractive to be entirely modern. Although I can find no recorded history of it being used much more than fifty years ago, we must assume that variations of it have been practised since the dawn of commerce.

Nutrilite Products

The earliest example of an MLM operation set up in a form similar to that seen today – a carefully structured and fully documented marketing plan with a detailed contract between the company and the distributor – is Nutrilite Products of California, one of the first companies to develop the market for food supplementation products. During the 1930s, Nutrilite's preparations were being distributed by direct sales methods. Some of the most successful distributors began to realize that they had been instrumental in significantly improving the company's turnover and profit by introducing many of their friends and acquaintances to the retailing business opportunity that Nutrilite Products offered. This had, of course, been the result of extra effort on the part of the distributors concerned, but they did not receive any additional reward for assisting the growth of the company's business in this way. This inequitable situation was resolved by the company giving a 2 per cent bonus to each distributor who introduced any other distributors, based on the total sales of those distributors introduced. It was a very primitive system, but it achieved the basic aim of rewarding distributors proportionately according to the contribution they made to the overall profits of the company.

Amway and Shaklee

Nutrilite Products prospered until the 1950s, when it began to suffer from a number of internal management problems. These had a deleterious effect on the businesses of all their distributors and, as the decade came to an end, distributors who had built up the largest organizations within Nutrilite over ten years were becoming increasingly concerned for their future. They were also anxious about the future of the people they had brought into the business, to whom they had promised a secure and profitable opportunity. In 1959 two men split from the company, with their group of distributors, and planned the birth of a new company. They intended to give their people the security and profitability that had been hoped for with Nutrilite, and took the opportunity to plan carefully a detailed commission structure which would reward their people in exact proportion to the profits their efforts produced for the company. Richard DeVos and Jay Van Andel called their company Amway, and it is now the largest MLM company in the world. At about the same time, another ex-Nutrilite distributor was also making provision to build a new and secure MLM business. This person was Dr Forrest C Shaklee, and his company, Shaklee, also developed into a multi-national company (although its UK subsidiary has now been acquired by Nature's Sunshine Products). Whereas Amway developed a completely different line of products from Nutrilite to start their new venture (household cleaning products), Shaklee remained committed to food supplements and nutrition products. Ironically, several years after these breakaways, the Nutrilite company was bought by the successful and expanding Amway Corporation and now provides one of Amway's basic product lines.

In 1969 the well-established UK direct selling company Kleeneze was looking at other marketing structures for its products, and was impressed with the methods used by the Amway Corporation in the USA. Consequently, in that year, the company brought into being what is believed to have been the first genuine MLM business in Europe. In 1973 Amway (UK) Ltd started operations in this country, followed in 1975 by Shaklee.

Pyramid selling

The continued success of Amway, Shaklee and other genuine companies in the USA operating similar sales structures did not go unnoticed by a number of unscrupulous businessmen. They realized that the multi-level concept, when manipulated away from the original intention of rewarding retailing success, could be used to make money from people without bothering too much about retail sales of quality products to a satisfied clientele. Thus 'pyramid selling' was born. Many variations on the theme were witnessed, some involving reasonable products and many not, but all were based on one or more of these ingredients:

- large entry fees extracted from people on the understanding that they would profit by receiving many similar payments from new entrants that they introduced;
- encouragement to purchase as large an inventory of products as possible at the highest discounts available, before obtaining orders from customers or other distributors, and with no refund policy;
- no written contract between company and distributor;
- no training in, or any real concern about, selling products to the public.

Many gullible people (and some not so gullible) found themselves persuaded into spending their life savings on entry fees and enormous amounts of products. After the initial excitement and dreams of wealth, they realized that they were incapable of selling all the products to customers, or of persuading others to join in the scheme, and stories of bankruptcies and garages full of unsold products became familiar.

Pyramid selling soon found its way to the UK and by the early 1970s the problems it was causing and the publicity it was being given prompted parliamentary action. The Pyramid Selling Schemes Regulations 1973 were drawn up to put a stop to the worst excesses of the pyramid operations prevalent at the time. They laid down in detail what was to be contained in any advertisements for such schemes, and what information should be included in certain documents issued by the promoters. They required written con- tracts to be provided to all participants, containing certain rights, such as termination without penalty and the possibility of having unsold stock bought back by the promoter of a scheme on termination of the contract. They imposed a maximum limit of £25 on the amount of money that could be accepted by anybody from a participant who had been in the scheme for less than seven days, and prohibited non-returnable deposits for goods. Training facili- ties were to be provided free of charge, as this was another area where promoters of pyramid schemes had abused participants.

The regulations were extremely effective in bringing to a close this unfortunate chapter in the development of multi-level market- ing, even though they were very rarely used against the problem promoters. By this time they had probably made their killing and were planning other fraudulent schemes. There were genuine MLM companies in operation throughout the time of the pyramids, and they took part in the Department of Trade and Industry's consultations about the regulations. They needed no substantial alterations in their systems to comply with the new rules; indeed, their operations were probably used as a basis for the new regulations.

The DSA

In 1965 several non-MLM direct selling companies formed the Direct Selling Association and drew up a code of good practice for direct sales. Kleeneze and Amway were among the first MLM members of the DSA, and in recent years the DSA's MLM membership has risen to a significant level; one-third of the companies in the DSA are now users of MLM structures.

An era of change

MLM has had a long, slow, uphill journey over the last fifteen years to build its reputation against the fears and prejudices of the majority of the population. We are now witnessing an era of change, in which more and more MLM companies are being formed, and where many established and newer companies are examining MLM methods for the distribution of their products and services. Many new direct selling companies are set up every year, and of those applying to join the DSA a large proportion are MLM companies. By far the majority of household and commercial water treatment systems being sold today, for example, are sold by MLM distributors, and, of all the new products which will become popular in the 1990s, many will be sold through MLM schemes. In addition, many more traditional products and services will start to be sold in the UK by means of MLM systems. Perhaps by the end of the decade the proportion of UK direct sales accounted for by MLM will have risen from its current (1988) level of 15 per cent to a figure much nearer the USA level of 50 per cent. This will bring with it more and more opportunities for the average person with above-average ambition to obtain significant wealth.

The future looks rosy for MLM and the (hard-working) people involved with it.

Summary points

1. MLM is a straightforward (but exciting!) marketing concept which is widely misunderstood and unappreciated as a serious, wealth-creating business opportunity.

2. MLM offers ordinary people without capital or experience the chance to build a highly successful business.
3. Like every other business, MLM can be operated fraudulently, but you can avoid these schemes by using the information within this book.
4. MLM is *the* business opportunity of the 1990s.

2: Advantages of an MLM Business

In this chapter you will find many reasons why you should consider an MLM opportunity, whether you are looking for:

- some extra pocket money
- a second or third income
- a profitable career in your own business
- extreme wealth
- early retirement
- charitable funds.

Anyone can do it

This is a crucial point. No experience, qualifications or references are necessary. Anything that could be quoted as a reason for not being able to be successful in MLM is in reality only a disadvantage. It may be a large disadvantage, but not large enough to prevent a person with enough determination from making it work. Some reasons used might be as follows:

Financial status If you examine the background of successful distributors you will find no correlation between the level of success attained and previous lifestyle. People who were millionaires in their own field have taken up an MLM business and done it again. People who could barely afford the starter kit, having no car or telephone, have become tremendously wealthy.

Age The proportion of successful distributors in each age group is probably the same as active, thinking adults generally throughout the population. Retired pensioners have made their final years the most comfortable and happy of their lives. Teenagers have made a dynamic start in the business and have ensured that they will never have to work for anyone else, or for more than twenty hours a week for the rest of their lives.

Handicap   Blind and wheelchair-bound distributors who were determined to make something special out of their lives have built up large and profitable businesses.

Sales experience   This is most definitely irrelevant to success in the business. Most of the highly successful distributors had no sales experience at all when they started out. It could even be a disadvantage.

Unlimited potential

There is *no* upper limit to the earnings possible in a genuine MLM opportunity. None of the marketing plans that I am aware of have any maximum income level for distributors, and this would in any case be self-defeating for the company, because the higher the income of the distributor force, the larger the profits of the company. For any good product line with mass-market appeal which is sold through an MLM scheme its market share is likely to be only a minute fraction of the total market for that kind of product. The potential for growth in MLM generally is therefore enormous, so for all practical purposes it is quite true to say that its income potential is unlimited. The only limiting factor is your own imagination. MLM has allowed hundreds of people worldwide to develop £1,000,000 pa incomes, and thousands more to reach millionaire status. You can join them *for certain* if you are willing to do what's required.

Risk free

The most common reason why people back away from starting their own business is almost certainly the financial investment required for premises, equipment, advertising, stock, and a thousand other things. If the person concerned is currently an employee of someone else there is the added worry of quitting a job which provides a regular income, small though it may be.

These problems are eliminated with an MLM business. If you

have chosen the company carefully, your greatest financial risk need be no more than the cost of the starter kit (maximum £75, but usually nearer to £25), and even this is refundable within a certain period of signing up. Unsold saleable stock will be bought back by the company at a minimum price of 90 per cent of the price you paid for it (this is a legal requirement) if you decide to quit at any time. The only possible loss to you on quitting your MLM business may be the value of any business aids which you may have purchased, such as equipment for assisting business presentations (board and easel), or for recording useful information at seminars, training sessions and rallies. These will in any case have been optional purchases and can probably be easily sold through the distributor organization you have left.

As you will have gathered by now, no drastic change of occupation is necessary when starting and developing an MLM business. Your life can proceed exactly as it did before you started, apart from the number of hours per week that you have decided to set apart for your new business. You have seen in the first part of this chapter how you can develop an extremely profitable business with a regular, if reasonably small, amount of commitment. You can slowly and confidently build your business in your spare time until you are absolutely confident about leaving your normal job.

Flexibility

I doubt whether any other business is as flexible as MLM. I have talked about a commitment of ten hours per week, but you can make it eight, fifteen, twenty; it's up to you. Nobody is going to make you do more or less than you make up your mind to do. What if you want to do six hours this week and twenty the next? It doesn't matter. This is not the best way to build a big business fast, but you can do it this way *if you choose*. This business fits around you; you do not have to fit around the business. You do not have to open and close for business at certain fixed hours, you simply arrange mutually convenient times to service your customers. You do not have to arrange cover when you go on holiday, as the business will look after itself. In fact, if you wish, you can take your business with you when you go away. You can sell products and sponsor people wherever you go (assuming your company has affiliates in the relevant country).

No boss

This needs no explanation to anybody who has one. Good bosses and bad bosses all control a third of your waking hours and most, if not all, of your income. In MLM, as in any other business of your own, the only person you have to answer to is yourself. This can actually be more difficult than answering to somebody else, but it is infinitely more satisfying for many people. Not only do you not have a boss in an MLM business, but you also do not have any employees. How many people have shrunk from the idea of building a large conventional business for themselves because of the problems of finding, paying, keeping, disciplining and sacking staff?

Remember, your sponsors are *not* your boss and have no control over the running of your MLM business. They are your advisors, helpers, motivators, and maybe also your friends.

Training, advice and assistance

If you want to build a large MLM business as quickly as possible you are going to need all the help you can get to avoid the mistakes that others made on their way to the top. You will find that if you are with a committed and responsible company you will have the opportunity, at very reasonable cost (or even free on occasions), to receive as much training as you need. Not only will the company provide manuals, tapes, videos, seminars and conventions for training and motivation in every aspect of your business, but your upline distributors will almost certainly hold regular training and counselling meetings and occasional 'rallies' where very successful distributors will tell you their stories of how they made it happen for them.

What happens when you set up in business in the conventional way? It is unlikely that you will have a unique product, so you will be in competition with every other supplier of similar products in the area. Your competitors will do all they can to obtain more business for themselves at your expense. If they can think of a great new way to sell more stock they will certainly not share it with you; indeed, they will probably do everything in their power to hide it from you. This will be the case even if your competitor is selling the same manufacturer's products. In MLM the situation could not be more different. Because of the unique character of the distribution structure it is always mutually beneficial for your sponsors or any of your upline to give you every possible assistance with your business. Your success is their success. It is profitable to help your downline – business is all about profits!

Time

Possibly the greatest benefit of a successful MLM business is that it can give you more of that commodity which everybody wants, and which is given in large quantities by the majority of people to someone else for most of their working lives. Many people have become very wealthy through their own business, whatever it may be, or even by being able to demand a very large salary for their employer for their skills, but how many of them have enough time at their disposal to fully appreciate what their money can do for them? How many can lie in bed until ten in the morning on a weekday if the fancy takes them, or pick their children up from school every day?

If you are working hard at some other occupation when you start your MLM business it may be a struggle to invest yet more time in another activity. However, it is an investment. When you invest money you expect a good return on that investment. You already know that there is no financial investment necessary in MLM, but what you do have to invest is *time*. Time invested now will repay you later at an exceptional rate of interest. You might want to spend forty hours a week in your MLM business, but it can be built profitably in twenty, fifteen, or ten hours a week. When the time is right you will have the opportunity to let your MLM business provide all of your income, leaving you with a great deal of the most precious possession you can have.

Security

What happens when you retire from a job after forty-odd years of service? A pay cut called 'a pension' rewards you for your efforts, and might be halved for your spouse if you happen to die first. What if you become unable to work at some point before you retire? You will get pay for six months if you are lucky, and maybe even half pay for another six months, then you're out, perhaps with a pension to allow you to struggle on for the rest of your life. Is this security?

Suppose you built up the most successful sales team ever known within a large conventional company. You helped to give them their best-ever profits and they paid you handsomely for it. Then you died suddenly and unexpectedly. How would your family be treated by the company? A nice lump sum and a reasonable pension, perhaps? A regular share of those big profits that continue to be made from your previous efforts? Hardly likely. Contrast this with a large and profitable MLM business built up by Mr and Mrs Smith with a good stable company. The bonus and royalty payments to the Smiths can be made part of their estate. If Mr or Mrs Smith dies the other continues to receive the payments. If they both die, the payments go to their heirs. If either or both are incapacitated (or they retire) their organization could still continue to grow and profit and provide the Smiths with the earnings due to them for building the sales network which continues to profit the company. This is more like true security.

I know some businessmen who cannot take a relaxing holiday because of worries about what is happening in their business while they are away. They would probably admit that they would rather stay at home for this reason. With an MLM business you can go away for a fortnight's holiday and come back to find that you have made more money in those two weeks than you did the previous month! You literally can make money while you sleep. Depending upon the size of your organization, you can be assured that, at any time of the day or night, ten, fifty, maybe two hundred of your distributors are showing the business to one or more people, and another five hundred are selling products. All of these are making money for themselves, and for you at the same time!

Earn what you're worth

The only way to be paid according to results is to work for yourself. Many employers offer very attractive commissions and per-formance-related pay, but can they really say they will pay you *exactly* what you are worth? MLM must be the finest example of a business which pays you in direct proportion to results obtained.

Many people ignorant of the fine details of MLM commission structures imagine that you can recruit one or two people, let them do all the work for you, and sit back watching the money roll in. If people really did just sit back, nothing would get sold, and no one would make any money at all. The task of an MLM company is to create a marketing plan which is firstly attractive to the new distributor planning to do some retailing. The next step is to make it attractive enough to encourage the sponsoring of new distributors so that reasonable wholesale profits can be made. Finally, there has to be an incentive to train and develop sponsoring distributors to the 'breakaway' point (where they deal directly with the company and lead their own group of distributors). This incentive will be in the form of a royalty payment based on the total sales of the breakaway group. The company does not want anyone to stop here, though. It wants to encourage continued expansion, and it will construct its plan so that a significant amount of business by a distributor, in addition to that of his breakaway groups, is necessary before royalties are paid out. The plan might be structured so that the royalty payment increases depending on the size of the distributor's other business.

All this means that the companies go to great lengths to develop a system which pays their people as closely as possible according to the continued effort they are making to build the business. You cannot make a lucky find of one or two superstar distributors and expect to be set up for life. Your income will always be proportional to your efforts.

A family business

This is a business that brings families together instead of keeping them apart. Husband and wife can contribute equally to the business, and the children can be involved too. Perhaps one partner will concentrate on retailing and the other on sponsoring. Because nobody needs any special previous experience to begin and develop the business, both partners will be able to put as much effort as they wish into it. This occasionally has dramatic effects on a spouse who has channelled full-time efforts into raising a family, and feels that previous skills have deteriorated with disuse. The opportunity to participate fully in the family business is often grasped with much enthusiasm.

In the beginning, when most time is being invested in the new venture at a period when full-time jobs are also being held down, it may not seem to be the best way for the family to see more of each other. The thought that tends to hold everything together through this tough period is that the family are working for a future when they will have more time together than they ever thought possible.

Some families have started their MLM businesses as partnerships of three or more people – father, mother, son and daughter, or any similar combination. If all partners commit themselves to building the business, imagine how fast the family income will increase with four people sponsoring! Even children can take a role in the business by taking orders, answering the telephone, making deliveries, and so on.

Few jobs and businesses offer this type of full family involvement. And when the time comes for recognition of successful distributors – the seminars in exotic locations, stage presentations, cruises – it is the family that is invited, or at least both partners in the business.

Do you want to move house every few years? Most people don't, especially once they have a family. Doing so can create very high levels of stress within the family of a company executive who is obliged to move house frequently in order to climb the corporate ladder. If you build a profitable MLM business you can live where you want to live and stay there if you want to. If you want to move, that's no problem; your organization can look after itself and you can go and live somewhere else, continue to build your organization there and receive income from both.

An international business

How would you go about expanding a conventional business internationally? It would be an understatement to say that it would not be the simplest of tasks, but let's see how it's done in MLM.

First, you must be working with a company which already operates in other countries or is about to do so. All the problems of starting up a large new business in a foreign country are taken care of by the company itself. When it is ready to supply your new foreign business with products and back-up it will tell you. All you need to do now is sponsor in that country and watch your new business grow! How do you sponsor abroad? Easy. Build yourself a large organization in the UK and tell them all to think about who they know in other countries. When they start sponsoring the people they know, by telephone, letter or personal visit, they and you benefit by international sales made by the new groups abroad. In addition you can take a tax-deductible holiday/business trip there yourself and sponsor as you would do in this country. It's as simple as that. Your foreign downline will be assisted by the company and other distributors in the country, and it may develop into a substantial size with very little input from you.

A ready-made business

People make other excuses for not starting out in a business of their own: What type of products will I sell? What sort of market is there for them? How would I advertise them? Who will make them? What's the best way to sell them? Am I doing everything legally? How do I expand my business? Where do I go for help? Will it work? What literature do I need? MLM is ready-made and waiting for you to start. Every conceivable problem has been examined and rectified in advance. The product range will have been test-marketed and there will be a definite section of the marketplace ready to buy the goods. The production, packaging, supply, accounting, payments, legalities, literature, sample packs, and so on, should all have been taken care of, leaving you free to get straight into the development of your business without any of the usual doubts and challenges clouding the primary issue of moving the products.

If the company has been around for any length of time there will be a wealth of information available through the distributor network to advise and assist new entrants in every aspect of building the business. Your starter kit will contain everything you need to get straight into the nitty-gritty of building your own business. The only thing not included is people, which of course is where you come in. Can any other business be this easy to start?

Franchising is often compared to multi-level marketing, and is commonly quoted as being one of the best business opportunities of the 1990s. There is, no doubt, a wealth of opportunity in this field, and of course it also offers a 'ready-made' business, but how much money will you need before you can get it off the ground? Many thousands of pounds for a fast-food outlet, for example. An MLM business costs £75, *maximum*. How much scope are you given for developing the business in your own way, as opposed to the strict and comprehensive detailed procedures laid down by the franchisor? Do you want the problems of employing people? No employees are necessary with MLM. Finally, will they accept you? They do not give out franchises to the first person who asks, and there may be some qualifications and references to supply before you get a look in. Anyone can start an MLM business.

Recognition

When was the last time your boss told you what a great job you'd done? Or told someone else what a great job you'd done? Or let it be known in any way what an asset you were to the firm? If you can put a date on any of these happening in the last six months then you are in a small minority. Most employees find that their managers and supervisors only comment on their standard of work when they make a mistake of some kind. When you do well in MLM you know it, and so do as many other people in that company's organization as possible. You will (or should) not be criticized for under-performing; your own conscience is the only judge of that. But if you reach any of the numerous levels of achievement set up in the scheme, however minor, your achievement will be recognized for what it is: the successful attainment of a goal set by you.

You may be awarded with a badge or certificate, you may be mentioned in the company's newsletter or magazine, you will be properly recognized as an achiever and an example to others. None of this is compulsory, though! If it all seems childish to you right now, you are perhaps underestimating the importance of recognition of achievement in every aspect of a person's life. Recognition is a spur to greater achievement and endeavour, and an inspiration to others. It is also one of the best forms of reward for effort, often more important than money for some people. Apart from the personal satisfaction of being recognized, it is purely and simply good business practice. It motivates people and keeps them happy and is therefore profitable.

Helping people

How much help could you give someone right now to improve their quality of life? With a good MLM business you hold in your hand an opportunity, to offer to anyone who needs it, which can improve their situation as much or as little as they wish. Not everybody wants such a business. When you can give it to someone who wants it and needs it, and can give them all the help and guidance they need to reach their goals in the business, you will be helping that person more than you ever thought you could help anybody. I know it's profitable to help others build an MLM business, but does that make it any less satisfying, or detract from the benefits gained by the other person?

An infallible business

I do not mean to imply that everyone who starts an MLM business will become wealthy. You have read that the financial risks in starting such a business are virtually non-existent, so there is no question of the venture failing, leaving you in debt. The facts are that with commitment, persistence and consistency (and a few other qualities), you *will* build a large profitable business. No question about it. A time scale cannot be laid down for the growth of the business – that depends on any number of variables – but you *will* reach your goals if you practise the three rules above. In the long term there is no luck involved, although you may gain a bit and lose a bit along the way. There are no circumstances which can affect the eventual outcome if you do what is necessary. In this respect you cannot fail. The choice is quit or succeed. Quit and nothing changes; don't quit and you will succeed.

No territories

In MLM there are no exclusive areas of operation for distributors as there would be for the salespeople employed by a large company. You may sell to anyone, anywhere, and nobody is going to interfere.

Charitable fundraising

MLM can be utilized extremely effectively as a fundraising method for clubs and charities, regardless of any desire amongst the supporters of the organization to develop their own business. For further details on how this can be done, *see* Appendix I.

Early retirement

If this is what you want, you can have it through MLM, if you put in the necessary work beforehand. Early retirement in a job usually means somewhere around the age of 55, without a great deal of continuing income (half your salary?). In MLM it can mean 45, 35, even 25, and an enormous income. Retirement means just that – you need do no further work at all and you can continue to reap the rewards of the profits made by the (extremely) large sales network which you have worked so hard to build. Most good schemes offer a retirement option after the development of a certain size of organization by any distributor. You would have to work very hard to get to this stage, in any of the schemes, but it is perfectly possible within ten years, and maybe only five years for exceptional people.

There are probably dozens more special advantages of having an

MLM business, but just these must have convinced you that choosing MLM for a part-time money-spinner or for a long-term business career is an eminently sensible step to take.

Summary points

1. *Anyone* can do MLM, without risk and with full, free training.
2. *You* are the boss in your MLM business, not your sponsor or the company (reasonable rules and regulations aside).
3. Unlimited earnings and the time to enjoy them are available through MLM.
4. You really can 'grow rich while you sleep' by building an international business and receiving substantial incomes 24 hours a day from the efforts of people worldwide, who are part of *your* business.

3:   How it Works

In this chapter you will find out:

- exactly how MLM works;
- how a highly profitable business is developed;
- about the different types of MLM schemes and how the concept can be abused.

Defining multi-level marketing

Before you read any further you should know exactly what I mean by 'multi-level marketing'. A very basic definition could be as follows:

'A method of selling goods directly to consumers through a network developed by independent distributors introducing further distributors, income being generated by retail and wholesale profits supplemented by payments based upon the total sales of the group built by a distributor.'

When you start showing interest in this subject you will come across many schemes which purport to be multi-level marketing. What you should bear in mind is that, like any other form of business, the concept of MLM can be used and abused. The theory behind it is such a powerful marketing tool that it has been tried in every different form imaginable. Some of the variations will be discussed at the end of this chapter so that you can see how the concept can be adapted, and so that you can make up your own mind about what 'proper' MLM is. I will also show you how the concept can be abused in order to attract the people who think it is possible to profit without supplying any form of goods or services to anyone. But first I need to describe the development of a genuine MLM business, step by step, to show you how it can provide you with a substantial income by the diligent application of a small amount of selling and some duplication of the principle.

How multi-level marketing works

In the first chapter I discussed the theory of MLM and the basic set of principles behind it, how it could benefit you and the way it has enabled people to create a substantial income for themselves. Now for some hard figures, some arithmetic to make the principles understandable. Don't skip to the next section if you're not fond of numbers; the calculations are simple, and surprising!

Sponsoring

First of all . . . you are 'sponsored'. This means you are now in business for yourself (but not *by* yourself, as you will see), having signed up with a company whose products you will be distributing. Your sponsor is an existing distributor, unless you are one of the first few distributors sponsored directly by the company at the outset. He or she is either the person who has introduced you to the particular company and its business opportunity, or the person nominated by the company to sponsor you following your initial approach to them as your chosen MLM company. Your sponsor and his or her sponsor, and everyone 'upline' from you, will benefit from your success and will therefore be available to give you every possible assistance in the building of your business.

Signing up

You pay an initial fee to be enrolled as a distributor, which will probably cover a complete set of company literature: a sales manual, a regular newsletter or magazine, product information, order forms, business advice, and maybe product samples. The maximum amount of money which may be accepted by the company from you within the first seven days is set by law at £75. You will sign a contract which binds you to abide by a set of rules regarding your conduct as a distributor. (The company obviously has to ensure that its reputation is protected as well as that of its distributors, and that the business is run on legal and ethical principles.) It also binds the company to supply goods and commissions and provide such services as promised in the sales plan and literature so that you can run your business as efficiently as possible without undue difficulties. You are now able to purchase goods from the company at 'wholesale' price. Before I mention selling, let's suppose that you signed up only because you liked the company's products and you wanted to be able to buy them at less than retail price. This is a perfectly acceptable reason for signing up. The company and your sponsor should be quite happy with this as they will profit, however insignificantly, from your participation. Your benefit will be your savings on the products you use. If your usage of the products amounts to £50 retail value per month and the basic 'wholesale' discount is, say, 20 per cent, then your business looks like this:

Profit on retail sales – £0 per month
Personal use savings – £10 per month (monthly purchase of
    £50 value of goods, costing you £40)

Retailing

Retailing the company's products is the first step towards extra income. The profit on the retail price is yours, and you can make a reasonable sum each month in this way, although there is always limit to the amount earned because of your own limitations of time. Suppose you retail £100 worth per month:

Retail profit (£100 × 20 per cent) =   £20 per month
                                    = £240 per annum

The methods of selling vary depending on the type of product or service, your own personal preference, the company's recommendations, and a multitude of other factors. A large proportion of all direct sales are on a person-to-person basis, initiated by referral, recommendation or straightforward approach. Your company's literature will provide all the information necessary to start building up a customer base in the most effective and efficient way. They will supply you (for a small fee – this is business, not a charity!) with customer receipts, leaflets, advertisements, samples, order forms, invitations, video and audio tapes, product accessories and so on.

Product distribution

In most cases you will have been sponsored by someone living near enough to you to supply you directly with all the products and sales aids. It will be your responsibility to pay for your products when ordering, and to collect them from your sponsor. Sponsors receive products from their sponsors, and so on. A distributor with a monthly order (business volume) above a specified level will be able to order products direct from the company, who will despatch them by road (normally) to the distributor. The goods will then filter through the network, ending up with the customer. Some modern companies will supply all goods by mail to each individual distributor. By these methods, no stockholding of products is necessary. The distributor may be out of pocket from the time of ordering stock until receipt of the goods and delivery to the customer. It is always good business practice to operate on a 'cash on delivery' basis with the retail customer, and usually it will take only seven to ten days to complete the sale. However undesirable it may be to hold large stocks of product – using up space, tying up cash, and for other reasons explained later – it makes sense to hold a minimum inventory in order to supply customers immediately, where possible, with your best selling lines.

Many thousands of people are content to make a useful extra income by retailing alone, within an MLM scheme.

Discounts

Increased discounts become available as monthly sales increase. In this theoretical example the distributor's discount on the retail price rises to 25 per cent when the monthly order reaches £250 retail value. This discount is given on the *complete order*. It will either be given directly when making your order, or at a later stage as a separate monthly payment after paying a standard 'wholesale' price for the products.

Now we can suppose that your retailing has reached £250 per month

Retail profit (£250 × 25 per cent) =   £62.50 per month
                                              =   £750.00 per annum

The company in this example has a scale of discounts which increase as your monthly business volume increases. It looks like this:

Business Volume £	Discount %
less than 250	20
250+	25
500+	30
1200+	35
2500+	40
5000+	45

(At this point I should explain the method of simplification which I am using in this example. The above table shows business volume in 'pounds worth' at retail price. If this scale was retained over the years, inflation would alter its meaning. As prices rose, it would take less effort to reach each level. Instead of changing the business volumes to rectify the situation, many companies instead allocate a numerical point value to each product which remains the same as prices alter. It is therefore possible to retain the discount table figures precisely as they were to begin with. Rather than make the examples unnecessarily complicated I have stuck to 'retail value in pounds' for the business volumes. The principles behind the calculations remain the same.)

You have done pretty well personally to retail £250 worth. Is it going to be possible to double your own sales so that you receive 30 per cent discount? Maybe. The higher levels of discounts are, however, going to be very difficult, if not impossible, to achieve alone.

Developing a network

Developing a sales network is the way to substantial earnings in MLM. Your efforts in building up a distributor organization for the company's products will be rewarded by discounts, bonuses, royalties and other incentives in direct proportion to your success – in other words, the sales generated by distributors in your group. You can only service a finite amount of customers on your own, so in order to develop your sales organization you must *duplicate* your business in order to reach out to more customers. A good company will provide you with advice on the best methods of developing your group, and show you their recommended way of presenting the business opportunity to others through business aids such as information packs and video films. Some of the best advice will be available from within the distributor group of which you are already a part. The most successful distributors will ensure that their experience and expertise are available to everyone in their group.

Some profits and earnings

Let's see how your profits can develop when you start to build your business. I am going to assume that you, and everyone else you sponsor, manage to make retail sales of just £100 per month; this figure should be easily achievable by most people. A certain period of time after commencing your new venture you will have succeeded in bringing in, say, six new people whom you have helped to get started and who are now also retailing £100 worth per month (*see* Chapter 5 for how to sponsor). Your business now looks like this:

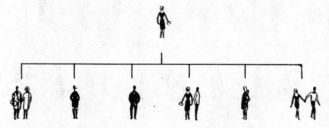

Figure 1 You and your 'first level' of distributors

Your total group volume is now £700, allowing you to purchase at 30 per cent discount from your sponsor (*see* the table on p. 42). Your six 'downline' contacts purchase from you at 20 per cent basic discount, so you will retain 10 per cent of each of your distributors' volume. Now look at your income:

Retail profit (£100 × 30 per cent)   =   £30
Wholesale profit (£100 × 10 per cent × 6) =   £60
                                           =   £90 per month
                                           = £1080 per annum

If you continue to build your business your earnings start to increase dramatically. You will have taught your downline contacts to duplicate their business as you have and they, for the purpose of this example, have each successfully introduced three more people who wish to start as distributors. There are now 25 independent businesses in your group, all retailing £100 a month. To develop a group of this size, all retailing steadily, you will have had to put in a reasonable degree of consistent effort, and this effort now begins to pay off handsomely. This is your group now:

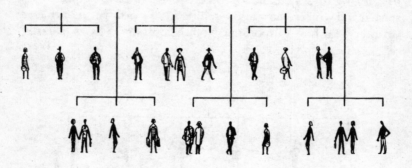

Figure 2 Your organization with two levels of distributors

Your business volume is now £2500 enabling you to purchase at 40 per cent discount. Each of your personally-sponsored distributors (often called your 'first level') now has a group volume of £400, enabling them to buy from you at 25 per cent discount. This means that you retain 15 per cent of your first-level distributors' group volumes. Your income can now be calculated as follows:

Retail profit (£100 × 40 per cent)   =   £40
Wholesale profit (£400 × 15 per cent × 6) = £360
                                        =   £400 per month
                                        =   £4800 per annum

Consistency and commitment for several hours a week will produce
rapidly increasing earnings. In this example you continue to help
and motivate your group to duplicate the business. We'll assume
that your second-level distributors manage to assist only two new
people each to start and develop a business of their own. Let's see
how the picture looks now, with everybody retailing £100 per
month:

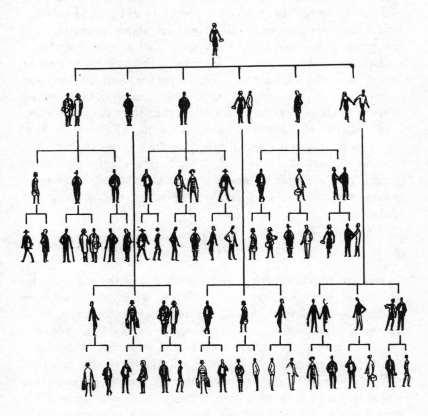

Figure 3 Your organization with three levels of distributors

With 61 distributors in your group your business volume has increased to £6100, giving you the maximum discount of 45 per cent. Each of your first-level distributors now has a group volume of £1000, enabling them to purchase from you at 30 per cent discount, leaving you with a retained discount of 15 per cent. Earnings are now thus:

Retail profit (£100 × 45 per cent)	=	£45
Wholesale profit (£1000 × 15 per cent × 6)	=	£900
	=	£945 per month
	=	£11340 per annum

You should bear in mind that when you started your business you were allotting perhaps ten hours a week to it, balanced between selling and sponsoring. Throughout the above example, your commitment has remained at ten hours a week. How long has it taken you to make £11340 per annum by working ten hours a week? It will depend on you, on how much you put into your ten hours and how effectively you use them. It could take you two months or ten years to reach this income, but if you're consistent you'll get there.

You should also bear in mind that the model above is a tidy, symmetrical diagram which is totally unlike any real-life network, because of human nature and the differences between people generally. While some will sponsor many more than I have shown, others will do less, while many will retail only or drop out altogether.

Royalties

By now you may be thinking that there is a flaw in the system; if the network keeps growing, what happens when your first-level distributors are able to claim 45 per cent discount from *you*, when you are already on the maximum discount? Do you lose all of your wholesale profit? The answer must be 'no', otherwise MLM would not do what I have already told you it will do. This is what happens.

When you reach the top discount level you will be collecting £5000 worth of stock from your sponsor each month, which is a considerable amount of product. At this point a separate system is needed, otherwise the whole operation would become unmanageable because of the quantities of stock being handled. When this level is reached (perhaps for a number of consecutive months) your sponsor ceases to be your supplier and you will deal directly with the company, who will deliver direct to you. If the company is one that supplies direct to all distributors from the start, you are still going to arrive at the situation where your first-level distributors reach the maximum discount level at some point. Similarly, this situation will occur with your first-level distributors as they reach the £5000-a-month level.

At the top of the discount table a distributor 'breaks away' from his sponsor and the sponsor then loses that distributor's group volume from his own 'personal group volume'. You will expect some reward for your efforts to replace the wholesale discount you had been receiving, and to make it worthwhile continuing to develop your organization. This reward comes in the form of a bonus payment from the company, probably calculated as a percentage of the total business volume of each of your 'breakaway' groups which have qualified at the £5000 level. For this example the bonus will be 5 per cent.

Referring back to Figure 3, your group became a breakaway group at a monthly volume of £6100. Assume then that when your six first-level people breakaway, it will also be at £6100 per month. This will of course not happen overnight; you will have to put in a substantial amount of effort to help your group build their businesses, and the time it will take depends on the concentration of that effort. You have now lost your wholesale profit on the sales made by your six first-level distributors, but it has been replaced by the 5 per cent. This gives you:

$$£6100 \times 5 \text{ per cent} \times 6 = £1830 \text{ per month}$$
$$= £21960 \text{ per annum}$$

This is twice the income shown in Figure 3, but there's more to come. I have not taken into account the fact that you are continuing to sponsor, in your ten hours a week. You didn't sponsor six and then stop, you carried on showing your business to people and bringing some of them into it. So in addition to your six breakaway groups you now have many more first-level distributors, new groups developing with your help, and more wholesale profit being retained by you. It would therefore not be an exaggeration (it may actually be an understatement) to assume that the income from the developing group pictured in Figure 3 is still being received at the stage you have now reached. Your income is now therefore:

£1830 + £945 =   £2775 per month
                 = £33300 per annum

And this is still not the whole story. Further bonuses are almost certainly available from the company: to encourage you to develop more breakaway groups; to encourage you to help and motivate your first-level distributors to develop *their* first level (your 'second-level'); to encourage you to sponsor more and train your people to sell more. Any number of differently calculated bonus schemes may be available, and they will usually be financed from funds set aside by the company for that purpose from the profits on sales made nationwide. Some schemes pay bonuses only on a certain number of 'levels' of downline, and only on a certain number of personally-sponsored groups. Other benefits are usually available at various levels of achievement, and these might include free cars, travel, holidays, and business seminars in exotic locations. For our last configuration shown in this example, a sum of £500 per month can realistically be added to the final income to take account of the additional bonuses accrued. Your earnings for your ten to fifteen hours per week are now approaching *£40000 per annum*.

Do bear in mind that I really am being conservative with the income figures I am quoting. £100 sales per month is extremely low for many people in MLM, and you could just as easily work out all the examples above based on £200 or £300 per month sales. The above figures are fine just for the purposes of an example, but in reality, if you are putting a great deal of properly-directed effort into the business, and teaching your organization well, the financial rewards you will receive will easily outstrip them. (You will read more about this in Chapter 8, where I interview some top-level distributors.) In fact, £40000 per *month* is not at all out of the question, if you are willing to do the necessary work.

Going full-time

At this point you may start to think that time spent on any other occupation could be used to more advantage in your MLM business.

After all, if ten to fifteen hours a week can produce the sort of income shown above, what will twenty hours a week bring in? And that is still only half the average working week. Some people develop a gigantic business, and carry on with their original full-time occupation with the sole purpose of demonstrating to their organization and others that a substantial business really can be built in a few hours a week of a busy person's time. For those who have a job they love but a salary they hate, a successful part-time MLM business solves the problem. Most people who have built their MLM business to a substantial level, however, have no compunction about leaving their previous job as soon as possible. What is better than having your own business, working the hours you want to work, continually increasing your income, and enjoying it?

Retirement

Anyone who has put enormous effort into building up a substantial business over a number of years would expect to be able eventually to put someone else at the helm, and spend a number of years in comfortable retirement on the continuing proceeds for which they had worked so hard. If their business reaches the necessary size, this option is quite possible. And it is the same with your MLM business. At a certain level, in most schemes, there is certainly an option to retire while still drawing the benefits of the large sales organization that you have worked so hard to develop. Your organization will be large enough to grow without any further input from you, and your income is therefore likely to continue to increase steadily.

Having said that, the retirement option is not one taken up by the majority of successful MLM practitioners, mainly because they thoroughly enjoy what they do and find it to be a more worthwhile activity than anything that they have ever done before. This fact is borne out by the number of very wealthy distributors who continue to put great efforts into their businesses even though they have more than enough money coming in. They continue with their business for enjoyment and the opportunity to help other people realize *their* ambitions.

Variations on the MLM theme

What I have told you so far about MLM is based on the largest and most sophisticated companies, who run schemes in which the top priority is quality, value-for-money products being sold to retail customers by every distributor, balanced with sponsoring of further distributors in order to build up a solid and secure business. There are variations on this theme; for example, the ratio of sponsoring to selling by the average distributor can change. It might be recommended that selling the products should be given a higher priority than sponsoring, whereas in another scheme it may be usual that a lower average level of sales is allied to a much greater sponsoring rate. Either way is fine; the second method produces the same sales figures but involves many more distributors. These are the types of operation which I suggest give the best opportunity to build a solid, secure and lasting business. We can now examine some other types of MLM.

Distributor-targeted networks

It is obvious that the purchase and use of an MLM company's products by the distributors in the network is an essential part of any scheme. It is not usually compulsory but of course it is good common sense. All types of business people use their own products whenever possible. In MLM the benefits are:

- experience of the products increases the distributor's knowledge of them which is conducive to more confident and authoritative (and therefore easier) selling of the products;
- significant use of the products inspires duplication by a distributor's downline, creating higher business volumes for all concerned.

Many companies, perhaps recognizing the reluctance of many people to involve themselves in any significant amount of selling, have constructed schemes in which the basis of the business is purchases by distributors for their own use. Selling to retail customers is not discouraged but the principle behind the scheme is a commitment by each distributor to buy a certain quantity of products during a certain period for as long as he remains in the scheme. This is all perfectly legitimate, although to be successful the product has to be one that people will actually *want* to purchase regularly without feeling that they are doing so purely for the benefit of their upline. I have said that successful MLM *always* relies upon good products bought by satisfied customers. This applies whether or not the customers are the participants in the scheme.

Incomes from distributor-targeted networks cannot approach those gleaned from a retail customer-based network of the same size, not only because of the far greater number of product users but also because retailing distributors are supplementing their commissions with sometimes very significant retail profit. Many people, however, prefer this type of MLM business for reasons of their own, and there is no doubt that good incomes can be obtained if enough people are involved and the product is purchased regularly by the participants.

An additional 'benefit' which is given in some schemes is the opportunity to make a profit purely on the introduction of new participants, whether or not they prove to be successful, by means of discounts on 'starter kits'. As long as this aspect remains a minor part of the incentive to join a scheme these types of schemes are quite legal, provided that all the other relevant regulations are followed. There is nothing to stop a number of the variations outlined above being incorporated within the same scheme.

Other networks

The types of MLM business I have described so far have been those schemes introduced by a manufacturer or supplier and developed by their network of distributors for the purpose of selling that manufacturer's or supplier's goods. This is how the vast majority of MLM schemes in existence work.

An inevitable development of the basic MLM concept has been to create an MLM network which is not committed to distributing any one company's products. The scheme's promoter offers a multitude of different types of goods from different sources to the distributors, who may pick and choose which items appeal to them. Commission structures are calculated by the promoter for each type of product offered. The network may be built up by the circulation of a periodical; this not only acts as a recruitment aid but contains all the details of products available through the scheme. The fee for the periodical provides commission to distributors in the network. This type of scheme has the serious disadvantage that comprehensive distributor support, genuine customer guarantees and product reputation and reliability are unlikely to be forthcoming because of the varying and possibly dubious origins of the products.

In another type of scheme the 'product' is information, usually a publication of some description, often connected with business opportunities and advice. Its distribution is partly facilitated by the efforts of subscribers, who are paid a percentage of the subscription of any new subscriber they introduce. They may also be paid a percentage of further subscriptions obtained by the new subscriber, and so on, for a certain number of levels. This may be arranged in such a way as to comply with the relevant regulations, although it is perhaps questionable whether such schemes could be classed as serious business propositions. Some of these magazines encourage multiple distributorships which, in my view, is not the way to build a highly successful and stable business.

Chain letters

Step by step the concept can develop further and further away from genuine products and retail customers. The final step is to remove the products entirely! You now have what is commonly known as a 'chain letter' or 'fundraising club'.

You receive a letter inviting you to take part in the 'multi-level marketing' scheme by sending £5 to each of four people listed in the letter. You may be told that this payment is actually for the purchase of goods (usually some fiftieth-generation copies of various 'reports'), but these are superfluous to the main intention. After sending off your £20 you are then entitled to put your name in the number 1 position on the list. You make as many copies as you wish of the letter and the new list (say 200) and post them out to whoever you wish. The cost of postage, stationery and copying could be £40. What is then supposed to happen is that a percentage (say 4 per cent or 8 people) of the recipients of your letter will each send you £5, making £40. These 8 people will then send out letters, with your name at second position on the list, to another 200 each, and the same response means that you will receive 8 × 8 × £5 = £320. From the next batch of mailings from these 64 people, you would similarly receive 512 fivers, or £2560. Finally, your name is fourth and last on the list when 4096 people respond to the letters, making you a grand total of £23400.

There is nothing wrong with the theory here, but can it really work? I decided to do some market research on the subject and sent questionnaires to every name on every list on every chain letter that I came across. No one had made any money from participating, although one or two had just covered their costs. Most replies stated that the whole enterprise was a complete waste of time and effort. So what is wrong with the system? My guess is that the average response rate from the mailings is so low, probably far less than 0.5 per cent, that there is no hope of recouping the investment unless every person involved sends out staggering amounts of mail. Another point about chain letters is that they are so susceptible to fraudulent manipulation, and this is probably another reason why nobody seems to make any money from them. It is the easiest thing in the world not only to put your name at the top of the list before you send out your mailings, but also to put it (in the form of various aliases) in positions 2, 3 and 4. If everybody did this, nobody's name would survive beyond the first mailing. Finally, how many people decide to save their initial £20 by not sending for the 'reports' from the four people on their original list? If everyone did this there would be millions of letters circulating but absolutely no money! My guess is that the only true winner in a chain letter scheme is the Post Office!

Although the multi-level principle is used in all the above schemes, the basic difference in genuine MLM is that, at any particular time, everybody is benefitting. Every distributor who has sold a product has a satisfied customer and a profit. If nothing is sold nobody loses out. Starter kits and product inventories are refundable. Chain letters (if they ever work at all) can only provide profits to a number of people if a far greater number of people are in a loss situation, albeit temporarily.

I am not going to comment on the morality of chain letters. You may think that people are quite capable of making up their own mind about such a venture, or you may take the view that people are being misled by the glowing testimonials accompanying the letters. Personally, I think the best use of them is to collect recipes (have you heard of a 'recipe tree'?). The facts are: mathematically, they can work in theory, but they appear to come within the constraints of the Fair Trading Act and the Pyramid Selling Schemes Regulations, whilst invariably contravening them. They have also been held to be lotteries and are therefore illegal under the Lotteries and Amusements Act 1976.

Every possible combination and permutation of the above schemes exists, and sooner or later you will be approached in person or by letter to take part in one or more of them. You must examine what is on offer and make your own decision, hopefully based partly on the information you will find in this book. This book, however, is based upon building legitimate, secure businesses with the type of MLM described at the beginning of this chapter.

Finally, a large number of financial services firms work on the principle of multi-level structures, but they are not included in this book because of the basic differences between them and MLM companies dealing in goods. The selling of financial services requires special knowledge and, probably for this reason, people usually start off full-time. The introduction of new people is not normally suggested at the start, and average sales tend to be far greater per person than in the type of MLM discussed here.

Summary points

1. There is always a limit to how much profit one person can make alone. There is no limit to the profits that can be made by duplication of that person's efforts. Every big business is based upon duplication.
2. Like every other business concept there exists every conceivable variation of the MLM principle. Know the difference.
3. Chain letters don't work! Large, secure incomes can only be legitimately obtained by constantly providing goods and services to satisfied customers.

4: Making the Decision

The information contained in this chapter will help you to decide which multi-level marketing scheme to participate in. The chapter covers:

- where, and where not, to seek advice;
- questions to ask yourself;
- questions to ask about the products;
- what aspects of the companies to consider;
- what to look for in the marketing plan;
- how to choose a sponsor.

First, are you going to participate in multi-level marketing at all? You may be asking yourself at this point, 'Can it really work?', 'Could *I* do it?', 'What will my friends say?'.

Let's bring the whole thing back down to earth. If you have read this far you will know that the answer to the first two questions is 'yes'. You may be reading this book as a result of having been shown the marketing plan of an MLM scheme by a friend or acquaintance. Perhaps MLM is a completely new concept to you: you are excited but dubious, attracted but apprehensive. Perhaps your potential sponsor is waiting for your decision, and his enthusiasm is overwhelming; perhaps he or she is a friend whom you would not wish to disappoint.

Stop right here and remember:

this is business;
the opportunity will still be there tomorrow;
there is nothing to lose.

It's your decision

This is business, *your* business, if you participate. In business *you* decide what's best for you. You must make your decision based upon your own thoughts, research and feelings, and therefore any enthusiastic friends must be disregarded for the time being. You are grateful for being introduced to such an exciting concept for increasing your income, but now you must ensure that, if you are going into MLM, you choose the company which suits you best.

Don't rush it

The opportunity will still be there tomorrow, next week, and even next year. If it isn't, consider yourself fortunate not to have taken it up. There is absolutely no reason for rushing your decision on whether to go into MLM and in which scheme you will participate. If the opportunity has been presented to you as one which is most attractive now but becoming less so as time goes on (the 'ground-floor' opportunity), it is quite possible that the scheme has a limited future. For a discussion about the commonly held view that 'getting in at the start is best', see Chapter 9.

Although you should not rush into a decision, you should be aware that there is good reason to avoid *excessive* delay. Your enthusiasm for the whole idea may begin to wane after a certain period if you allow the details of the opportunity to slip away from the forefront of your mind through inaction. If you are initially attracted to the possibilities of MLM, the following days should be dedicated to finding out whatever you need to know in order to decide which scheme is best for you.

Nothing to lose

There is nothing to lose, and everything to gain. It has to be said that, unless the whole concept of MLM or any aspect of it is abhorrent to you, there is every reason to have a go at it. Just suppose you could make it work? Isn't it worth a try? Very many people have achieved more than they would ever have imagined they could in this business. You might give up within a fortnight; you will go back to square one, and have lost nothing. Alternatively, you might surprise yourself . . .

A cautionary note

Before going any further, I should give you a word of warning. Of course, you will want to talk to others about what you have seen and heard about a particular MLM business, to find out what they think. Most people, especially family and friends, are well-intentioned, but probably 80 per cent of the population have never heard of MLM, and maybe another 10 per cent have heard of it but don't quite know what it's all about. You must be careful not to treat opinions and advice from those people with more importance than they deserve.

You will probably discover that the majority of uninformed people do not have an especially positive attitude. Well-meaning advice to you may suggest that some people might be able to do it, but you aren't really cut out for that sort of thing. Such advice may destroy any amount of self-confidence that you do have, which may have grown spectacularly with the right nurturing. If you feel the need to discuss the subject in detail, find someone who really knows what they are talking about, like a successful multi-level marketing distributor.

Five aspects to consider

- you;
- the products;
- the company;
- the marketing plan;
- the people.

You

Having said previously that anybody can do this business, I will now say that you must of course *want* to do it. There is no point in wasting your own and other people's time by involving yourself in an MLM scheme as a favour to someone or to get someone 'off your back'. If you would rather die than try to sell something, forget MLM. Similarly, if you are one of those rare and fortunate people who is totally content with what you have and what you do, forget MLM.

Think carefully about you; it may be something you rarely do. Most of us would like more money, but not everybody is prepared to do more to get it. If you are prepared to work harder to improve your lifestyle, there are few opportunities better than MLM for the returns related to effort expended. Your extra efforts must be channelled into an effective routine, however. It is no good (if you want a substantial income) saying you will work hard at the business 'when you get time'. Do you say to your employer, 'I'll come in when I get time'? Your time spent in your MLM business – perhaps ten hours per week – must be found somewhere. From the TV chair? Then your time must be allocated daily to your business. You must be consistent and persistent. Are you willing to do this?

Are you willing to learn new skills in order to make the money that you want? You must be prepared to put yourself in the hands of your sponsors for a while and do what they advise, even if you don't understand why at first. You will have to study new methods of dealing with people which will give you the results you want from your new business. Others may discourage you and tell you that you can't do it, even people who are close to you. Can you take all this in your stride, knowing that you are determined to do it despite them?

The products

Once you have decided that MLM is for you, and vice versa, the most important decision is what products you are going to deal with. You have a virtually unlimited choice and you must find a product or products with which you feel comfortable, which you actually like and would use on a regular basis and, most importantly, which you feel happy about selling. Once again, this is an area where you may be receiving an excess of enthusiasm from a potential sponsor. You should distance yourself temporarily from the razzmatazz of any presentation you may have attended and examine not only the type of products involved with that scheme, but also those available through other companies. You may find that there are products available elsewhere with which you would much rather deal, or you may find that another firm sells a superior version of the type of product initially demonstrated to you. Pay some attention also to the quality of the company's literature, particularly their sales aids. Does it present the sort of image with which you wish to be associated?

Do you feel that it will assist you greatly in your selling (and your sponsoring)?

The following aspects of MLM products need some careful consideration:

Quality and value An MLM operation is only as good as the product offered. It is nothing without good quality products. Cheap and nasty goods at very low prices may be good value, but the firmest foundation on which to build a solid business is *quality*. You can well do without regular returns for refunds and exchanges for faulty or unwanted goods. The price a customer pays is forgotten soon after the sale, but the quality of the goods is remembered every time they are used. Look at the packaging; is it eye-catching and professional-looking? Try out the goods if possible; do they feel good and work effectively? Are they made to a recognized standard (British Standards, government regulations, and so on)? Are they as environmentally-friendly as possible? Are they, or any of their ingredients, tested on animals? These aspects of the products could be very important to some of your customers.

Would *you* buy them? You will never successfully sell a product that you do not believe in yourself. If you are not sure whether you would use the products yourself, stop right there. Only by using the products can you gain the knowledge and experience of them which will enable you to talk to potential customers with confidence. Reading about them is not enough. In any case, what impression would you give to a prospective distributor if you yourself were not using the products you are suggesting they might like to sell? Apart from these reasons, regular product purchases by distributors improve the profits of everyone within the network.

The guarantee How good is it? Many companies now offer completely unconditional refunds or exchanges, some even on return of the empty package. Naturally, this is an extremely useful sales aid and tends to give some indication of the confidence that the company has in its goods. If you are looking at a product without a comprehensive written guarantee then you should also look further afield, as you will almost certainly find another company which does supply one with its products.

Repeatability If your product is of good quality, good value, *and* consumable, then every satisfied customer is a permanent part of your business. Every new customer therefore increases your turnover. Think about the types of products which customers will want to buy from you again and again, because they actually *need* them. Perhaps products which are more of a 'luxury' will be cut out of a customer's budget sooner than other types of products in times of financial stringency. A continual supply of new customers may be necessary to stabilize your turnover. However, 'luxury' products are usually more profitable per item than other goods. The choice is yours.

New products   How committed is the company to constant product development and updating? Your product needs to keep up to date and in tune with current fashions in consumer thinking and buying. A steady flow of new products for introducing to existing customers will improve profitability. If you develop a solid business with a reliable, quality company you may appreciate the opportunity to expand into totally new product areas with them when they have fully researched and developed them. A variety of product lines may be beneficial so that new and prospective distributors for your business have a greater choice of business types from which to choose. If your business is cosmetics and your prospect is excited by the MLM concept but would not dream of dealing in cosmetics, you have lost out to another company's distributor. If, however, you can offer businesses in a range of products you may be more likely to persuade that person to join you.

The other side of the argument is that a company which specializes in one type of product can pay more attention to its quality and promotion than one which has many different lines. It may also have a better chance of being regarded by the public as a specialist in its field. Perhaps it will be easier for you to become an expert on your product if you are dealing with only one type; you may prefer the greater simplicity of selling one kind of product. A company with a single product must still ensure through consistent research and development that the product remains fashionable and desirable and is of the highest standard.

Selling   It does not matter how a product is sold (as long as it is legal and in compliance with the company's terms and conditions), since for each type of product there will be a recommended method which has been found to be most effective by most of the company's distributors. You may find that you feel much happier with one particular method than another, for whatever reason. As an example, party-plan sales tend to be a very common and successful method of selling perfumes, whereas personal recommendation is likely to be the best way of selling washing powder and other laundry products. You may want to go door-to-door. Today's door-to-door consists of a personal introduction, the loan of a comprehensive brochure, and calling back in person after a day or two to collect any orders.

Sales to businesses are becoming more common in MLM. Usually the pricing structure of the products is based upon selling those products by retail to individuals, thereby precluding the amount of discounting sometimes necessary to clinch larger sales to businesses. However, this has not stopped distributors of all types of products successfully completing many trade sales. In due course more and more products will be sold through MLM schemes which are ideally suited to trade sales; at the moment a huge number of water filtration systems are sold in this way.

So, any acceptable selling technique can be used to sell MLM products. Certain methods will be better for certain goods or for certain people. Whatever type of goods you choose for your business, it is worth taking time to consider the recommended and alternative ways of selling those goods so that you are happy that your turnover is going to be at a reasonable level for the amount of effort that you expend.

The company

How are you going to satisfy yourself that the company which has the products and the marketing plan that you like best is going to provide you with a long-term career opportunity, efficient and effective administration and a positive and dynamic working environment? The answer is that you can never be 100 per cent sure of this with any type of company, MLM or not, however, there are some basic principles to look for.

The main causes of failure of MLM companies appear to have been:

- poor management due to lack of relevant experience and commitment;
- failure to effectively communicate with and motivate distributors;
- inadequate administration and product delivery;
- insufficient initial financing;
- products of poor quality or restricted market.

Sometimes the founders of a new MLM scheme will have a marvellous product or service, but will not have the experience to handle a fast-growing MLM organization properly. Conversely, people with solid experience of developing a large distributor organization do not necessarily possess the qualities required for ownership and administration of a company. It is very difficult to decide whether a new company has what it takes to stay the course, but an essential ingredient might be wide experience within the MLM industry, either as a successful distributor or as a principal of another successful MLM company. If the management team consists of more than one person with the relevant experience, so much the better. The longer the company has been around, the better the picture you will be able to get of the quality of the management. Delve into the company's history as far as you can and see what success they have achieved. The simple fact that they have been around for a long period of time is significant.

Of course, you do not want to involve yourself with a company which is not financially stable, especially if you are intending to develop a long-term business, but this is difficult to determine with a new company. If you want to make further enquiries into matters such as this, there are official channels for obtaining certain company information. There is no reason why you should not ask the company directly for any information which you feel would put your mind at rest about joining them. Will they supply you with a copy of their annual report? Is the company a full member of the Direct Selling Association? (For more about the DSA *see* page 63.) What kind of investments have they made in offices, warehouses and manufacturing? Do they manufacture their own products, or at least have total control over the quality of the production processes? What about new technology for efficient administration, distributor support services and sales and business aids? Have they produced a high-quality video and audio cassettes as recruitment tools?

You will want to know that the company management really does know *you* and care about *your* business, however small it may be, so talk to them. Telephone the head office and speak to one of the directors, or, if you are close enough, go and see them. The response you get may give you a good indication of the corporate attitude towards the 'little' distributor, and when you come away, your gut feeling will tell you something of what you need to know about the company. In the majority of instances you will encounter warmth, courtesy and efficiency, however, not least because it is sound business sense ('little' distributors can develop into 'big' distributors!), so get behind the 'hype' of the initial appearance of the opportunity, and look at the *facts*. Ignore promises and projections for the future and concentrate on what the company has actually done. No one has all the answers, but find out what you can and trust your own judgement. Remember that there is no way in which you can lose out financially unless the company folds. This rarely happens; you can protect yourself from it by taking two precautions:

- keep your expenses low initially so that you do not have to worry about past debts if you do find it necessary to change to another MLM scheme;
- **never** purchase more than the minimum amount of products necessary to run your business efficiently.

Membership of the DSA

In 1965 the activities of some door-to-door salespeople were causing bad publicity for direct selling. In order to improve the image of the industry five of the largest direct selling companies – Avon, Tupperware, Spirella, Betterware and Beauty Counsellors (none of them MLM companies – formed the Direct Selling Association with the intention of promoting a code of good practice for direct selling companies and their salespeople. In 1987 the code was revised and gained the endorsement of the Director General of Fair Trading. Among many other requirements, the code brought into force a fourteen-day period within which a customer could change his or her mind about a purchase, still much more than is required by law today.

The directors and managers of DSA member companies are able to attend seminars and conferences to share experiences and learn from the techniques of other countries' direct selling organizations. In this way, the standards of selling and administration within their business are continually improved.

In addition, the DSA follows good international practice by appointing an independent Code Administrator whose job is to oversee the proper working of the code. Any complaint which has not been resolved to a customer's satisfaction within 21 days is sent to the Code Administrator for his judgement, which is binding on the company. This avoids the high cost to a customer of pursuing a complaint through the courts. The DSA also promotes MLM to the media and the general public. Details of all member companies are sent to anyone contacting the DSA (as they regularly do, following articles on direct selling that appear in the national press).

There is a great deal of accumulated knowledge about MLM within the DSA. Its governing council consists of nine experienced managers and directors, and the present Director was a managing director of one of the UK's leading direct selling companies.

One of the best ways, then, of being assured of a company's stability and integrity is to find out if it is a member of the Direct Selling Association. It would be wrong to suggest that a company *not* in the DSA is necessarily suspect, but all DSA members have had their marketing plans, financial positions and overall integrity carefully scrutinized for compliance with the association's comprehensive code of conduct and have been observed in action for as long as is necessary (usually around 12 months) to satisfy the DSA Council that distributors and customers will get a good deal from the company.

Distributor numbers

I want to make a comment here on something which is sometimes quoted by companies – the number of distributors in their scheme. This figure can vary tremendously from month to month in any MLM company, for a variety of reasons. An exceptionally active distributor can create explosive growth in his, and therefore the company's, organization. Some companies have an annual distributor renewal programme (a small fee is usually involved) in order to remove from their records all 'inactive' distributors, or at least all those who are inactive enough to decline to renew their distributorship. This yearly purge can reduce the number of registered distributors by anything up to 80 per cent, and is quite natural. Most people who get into MLM do not do anything with it, and this is a fact of life for which you should be well prepared when you start your MLM business. Some companies require renewal 12 months after the distributor joins, in which case there will not be the drastic fall in numbers at one point in the year. Instead, the distributor roll will always include a large proportion of inactive people. The number of distributors with a company at any one time is, therefore, a worthless piece of information. What is more important is what those distributors are doing with their business. If you are doubtful of this, and your thinking includes such words as 'ground-floor' or 'saturation', you may find it helpful to look closely at Chapter 9.

The marketing plan

It is sometimes difficult to assimilate fully the complexities of any company's commission and bonus structure the first time you see it. If you have been at all inspired by the multi-level concept when it is first shown to you, your head will be filled with circles and lines and vague notions of 'more people equals more money'. Now you need not get too carried away by the potential of the concept itself, but examine the details of this company's particular marketing plan carefully. For example, is it fairly easy to understand and to explain to others? Read the operating rules and conditions for distributors and make sure you understand them and agree with them. You should pay particular attention to the following.

Retail profit

What percentage* profit are you going to make on each retail sale when you start? Anyone you sponsor is also going to be concerned

---

* A note about percentages, which many people (and some MLM companies!) calculate incorrectly. You can only have a percentage *of* something, ie the figure you start with. Percentage profit (or return on investment) is found by dividing the *amount* of profit by the original cost to you and multiplying by 100. Similarly, percentage discount is the *actual* discount divided by the full price, multiplied by 100. Therefore, if a product is £4 wholesale and £5 to the retail customer, you can either say that your *profit* is 25 per cent or that your *discount* is 20 per cent.

with this. Many people may only wish to develop a retail business, so this figure is particularly important to them. You want your total initial retailing profit to be a sum large enough to cover your operating expenses such as petrol, leaflets, meetings, postage, advertising, stationery and so on. You should be able to calculate roughly how much product you intend to sell each week and get an approximate income figure from this. Remember, too, that retailing profits quoted by companies are often calculated on a figure that is less than the actual retail price. VAT may be taken off first, and the remaining figure converted to whatever units the company uses to work out its commissions. When you hear '30 per cent discount', make sure you know from which amount the 30 per cent is calculated.

Higher levels of commission/discount

Examine how the commission structure is made up. How many commission levels are there? How much product will you and your group have to sell before you reach the highest level? How is your commission obtained? In many schemes all the retail and wholesale profit is pocketed directly by you as you will have purchased the products at your current discount entitlement. In other schemes the wholesale cost remains the same to all levels of distributor, and a 'performance' bonus scheme takes the place of the higher discounts. This bonus may be paid monthly from the company or through your sponsor. The only difference between these two methods is that in the latter you might have to wait a bit longer for your commission (but you get it all at once!).

Royalties and incentives

What are the royalty percentages, and what are the personal group sales volume requirements in order to receive the highest percentages? Do they seem reasonable and achievable? How many further incentive schemes are there to motivate you to increase the size of your network? You may find all sorts of oddly named extra bonuses and percentages being offered to tempt you to 'widen' or 'deepen' your organization, or to teach your downline better. Find out how these royalty payments and 'override' commissions are calculated and paid. Some plans will restrict payments to those based on sales down to your third, fifth or seventh, level. They may also make restrictions on the width of your network on which payments are made. For example, if payments are made on a specified network size of, say, four deep and seven wide, this means that the maximum qualifying sales volume is that produced by you, plus up to seven of your first level, plus up to seven of each of theirs, and so on. The maximum number of distributors included in the calculation is therefore $1 + 7 + 7^2 + 7^3 + 7^4 = 2801$. You can do quite well with an organization of this size! You can do even better, though, if there are no restrictions. Can you imagine developing a network of ten thousand distributors? It's possible.

Other plans will include the sales volume of your complete network in royalty calculations, and maybe even a proportion of the company's total national sales. If the company also operates in other countries you may be able to sponsor people abroad and benefit from royalties paid on the sales volume of your organization there.

When comparing commission structures, don't get too excited by those that appear to make it fairly easy to reach the top 'breakaway' levels by having a lower sales volume requirement. All this means is that when distributors in your network reach those levels and break away, your royalty payments will be less because the overall sales volume will be less. If the top discount level is easier to reach because of a lower sales requirement the company may be able to offer royalties on more levels of breakaway groups. Obviously, the top discount level must appear reasonably achievable to the new distributor, but the higher the sales volume required the larger the royalty cheques in the long run.

You will find also that most schemes offer even more incentives for exceptional retailing or sponsoring efforts, the highest group volume in the specified period, reaching certain levels in the scheme, and many other achievements. These incentives range from minor gifts, such as discount vouchers to use against the cost of a holiday, up to major awards, such as large cash payments, complete holidays and seminars in exotic locations, cars, and even houses. Naturally, your organization's turnover will have to be colossal in order for you to qualify for the major type of award, but remember that many people have done so, and the incentives are open to all.

Finally, what about the retirement option? Like any business owner, if you have spent a significant portion of your life working hard to build up a successful and profitable business there will come a time when you will want to ease up a bit, pass on the reins to somebody else, and relax in comfort on the continuing profits of the business. A successful multi-level marketing business should be no different, so if you are looking to build a long-term financially secure business you will want to investigate what facilities the company's marketing plan offers for eventual retirement. Don't expect to find much on offer in this respect unless you intend to work very hard for long enough to build an extremely substantial business. You would not expect any other business to provide you with a secure retirement unless you had built it to such a level, so don't expect it from an MLM business.

Ordering and delivery procedures

How will you obtain your products? One of the principal benefits of MLM to a company is the saving made in the distribution of products, because it is done primarily through the distributor network at a small cost to each distributor rather than through a large road haulage operation at a large cost to the company. In most cases your products will be initially supplied by your sponsor directly until the size of your orders necessitates delivery to you by some other means. Many companies, however, use different methods, particularly mailing products to distributors when the goods are suitable. Sometimes all supplies are sent by post, to distributors *and* customers.

If you plan to develop a large business, stretching the length and breadth of the country, you will certainly want to find out how the company deals with long-distance sponsoring. You will be sponsoring people from all areas, and they will not want to travel hundreds of miles a week to pick up products from you. Similarly, although you may feel that it is a good idea to see your long-distance downline fairly often in the early periods of their business, you will not want or be able to deliver products that far on a regular basis. You may also be planning to sponsor people living abroad, in which case you may not see them from one year to the next. What provision does the company you are considering make to overcome this challenge?

What you will also need to know is how quickly you can obtain products after making an order. Not only will this be very important to your customers, but you do not want to be in the position of having to keep large stocks of products for quick supply to customers because of slow or unreliable deliveries. Is there a minimum order value? If so, will you be able to, or want to, keep your orders up to this level? What about handling, postage and packing charges?

Rules of conduct

When examining the 'small print' on the agreement between the distributor and the company, there are a number of aspects to which you should pay some attention.

Is there a requirement for each distributor to attain a minimum amount or number of retail sales in order to be eligible for bonuses and commissions, so that everyone is required to do their share of the basic task of selling to the public? Does this matter to you anyway? Some companies make this a requirement because of their strong belief that there should be no shortcuts to success.

Is stockpiling prohibited? If not, people who can afford it will be able to purchase large stocks of goods at much higher discounts than those who are only able to order goods which customers have already requested. Because of legal requirements the distributor who stockpiles is able to demand reimbursement of most of the cost of the goods if he subsequently decides to resign as a distributor, so there is rarely any question of bankruptcy or any significant financial loss, unless the company itself becomes insolvent. This aspect may not bother you but I mention it because good companies do not encourage distributors to stockpile, and feel that all their distributors should have exactly the same opportunity, regardless of their financial position. Those companies will have introduced rules to guard against stockpiling.

What other rules and conditions are imposed upon distributors? You should always find a requirement to conduct your business with the highest integrity and in the best interests of the company. This requirement will be expanded to a greater or lesser extent, depending on the company. There may be specific rules against certain activities, concerning advertising products, selling products to retail stores, advertising for distributors, inviting prospects to meetings, presenting the marketing plan, dealing with customers, and possibly more. Read and digest the rules, and make sure you are happy with them, or with the lack of them.

Finally, are you satisfied that the presentation of the products, the literature and, most importantly, the marketing plan meet the relevant legal requirements? If there is any departure from the rules you should seriously consider whether the commitment of the company is sufficient to provide you with the reliable and stable back-up you will need for a long-term profitable business relationship. For the necessary information on the legal aspects of MLM *see* Chapter 10.

The people

So far this chapter has covered many important matters which you should consider or at least be aware of before signing up as a distributor with an MLM company. What has not been mentioned is people. MLM is a 'people' business. It is all about people – the people running the company, the people distributing the products, the people buying the products, and all those other people out there who comprise your future customers and distributors.

If you have not yet become an MLM person you are in a position of being able to choose your sponsors. The company of your choice will provide you with names of active distributors in your locality who will sponsor you. You must ensure that they are the type of people whom you can really get on with. They must have integrity and sincerity. You should be excited about the prospect of introducing other people to them. You want your bonus cheques on time. You want sponsors who are committed to the company and to you, who will not suddenly disappear to another company's scheme as soon as you start to get the ball rolling with the one you have chosen. You want good advice at all times, not encouragement to spend money 'investing' in large stocks of product for a bit of extra discount. You may not be able to satisfy yourself of all these aspects of your potential sponsors before you join them; you must ask them a lot of questions and rely on your intuition.

When you start your MLM business you should feel that you are part of a winning team, a 'family', of which all the members are working together for the common good. If you have not attended one of the local 'opportunity meetings' or 'counselling' sessions, I suggest that you go along to see the sort of people alongside whom you will be building your business. You are sure to be pleasantly surprised to find that they are . . . just like you; ordinary people with more than ordinary ambitions.

Summary points

1. There is every reason to start an MLM business; is there any reason not to? Your TV won't miss you for 10–20 hours a week.
2. Get your advice from people who *know* the subject.
3. The products are the most important part of any MLM scheme.
4. Investigate the company as thoroughly as possible.
5. Find the right sponsor for *you*.

5: Building a Successful Business

This chapter will help you lay the foundations on which to build your MLM business, including:

- before you start;
- budgeting your expenses and your time;
- getting off to a good start;
- qualifying people;
- inviting people;
- advertising;
- presenting your business to others;
- following up.

So, you've decided that MLM is for you, you've picked your products and your company, and you've signed up. Now what? The simple answer is, ask your sponsor or sponsors. They may have only a few days more than you in the business and may be even less knowledgeable than you about the company and the concept itself – especially if you have read this book and they haven't! This should not pose too much of a problem, because if you have been sponsored into a well-run distributor organization there will certainly be an experienced distributor in your upline who will be working 'in depth' to help his downline to become proficient. In addition to this, a good company will supply you with helpful information of their own on how to build your business. All the same, it is useful to have at hand a reference book which contains all the basics and which can be picked up immediately for instant advice on action for success. This chapter is intended to provide that advice, but first an important question must be answered.

What is 'success'?

Success is often thought of as being synonymous with financial wealth, but can an unhappy millionaire be said to be successful? There are plenty of people around who have a lot of money at their disposal but who cannot buy the things they want the most. There are also plenty of people of modest means who have everything they want in life; these are the really successful people. Success is not defined by financial wealth, although it is a part of the lives of many successful people. The *Oxford Dictionary* calls it, perhaps most accurately, the '. . . accomplishment of what was aimed at '. This is the essence of 'success', and it is especially true in multi-level marketing. Not everyone wants a gigantic business which earns them thousands of pounds a week and all the hard work that goes into building it.

The majority of people in the MLM business want a reasonable extra income to pay off some of their bills and to treat themselves with a few luxuries now and then. Some are satisfied with making enough money to cover the cost of the products they buy from the company, many are looking to be their own boss for the first time, and of course some are aiming to be very rich. MLM is flexible enough to be able to offer all these people exactly what they want. When someone decides what it is they want and proceeds to make that goal a reality, they become successful at once because, in the words of a famous inspirational writer, success is 'the progressive realization of a worthy ideal'. And the person who decides whether his ideal is worthy is that person himself. You have to decide what you want out of your MLM business, and when you have done so and you are working towards it, you are being successful. This chapter and the next will give you enough information to make you wealthy in MLM, if that is what you want. If you desire something less than that you can pick and choose which suggestions you implement in your business.

Nothing worthwhile is easy

MLM is *simple* but it is not *easy*. It is simple because a successful business can be built by repetition of an easily-learned presentation and some genuine enthusiasm about the products and opportunity that you have in your hands. It is not easy because the two all-important qualities for MLM success – consistency and persistence – require some serious effort to attain and put into practice. It is not easy because you will have to overcome a substantial amount of negative reaction, from all kinds of people, even some who are close to you. It is not easy because the growth of your business may not be steady, but is likely to rise and fall several times before it becomes stable. You will be disappointed by people you think are going to set the world alight in your business, but do nothing at all with it. There will be times when you think that the whole thing doesn't work at all and you might as well quit. Nothing worthwhile is ever easy. MLM works, for sure, but only if *you* work *it*. You set the targets for the success that you want and you can reach them if you do what you know needs to be done. There is no one who can honestly say about their MLM business, 'I did everything they told me I should do, but it didn't work.'

Planning

Getting organized

Get this into your head before you start doing anything: you are going to be running a *business*, a small one initially but a growing one. At some point you will have to organize it properly as every other successful business is organized. The easiest and most prudent time to do this is right now, before anything else. It need not be anything elaborate, but from the beginning you should be able to see exactly the financial position of your business – where you are making the most money, and where you are spending the most.

If at all possible, you should dedicate an area of your home to your business. It doesn't need to be much, but you need to have a space where you can 'take care of business', where you have all your records, where you can feel, and therefore act, businesslike. Get yourself some sort of filing system, however rudimentary, so that you can find any bit of paper you need without wasting time. Try to get hold of a desk and an office chair, perhaps picking them up cheaply at an auction. You will need some basic stationery, an expenses book, a card index system, address labels, envelopes, and so on. If you have a computer so much the better, as you can dispose of vast amounts of paper by putting all your records on it. Ideally your 'office' should have a telephone, as it is far easier to make a 'business' call from a place of business. It is useful and impressive to have some professional-looking headed notepaper and business cards; in many instances your company will supply you with such stationery at a reasonable cost. Keep a good stock of sales and business literature at hand; it can be disastrous to have a 'hot' prospect and then find you have run out of the pamphlet you promised them, with a week to wait for the next delivery.

The taxman

You can only control your expenses if you know what they are, and the easiest way to keep track of them is to keep them all to a separate bank account. In this way a record of most of your transactions will be available by means of your statements. If at the same time you keep detailed records of all your other expenses and wherever possible obtain receipts for expenditure and keep them with copies of customer receipts and bonuses received in separate monthly envelopes, then you will have everything that is necessary to keep the Inland Revenue happy.

Ideally you should tell your tax inspector about your new business the moment you start it; the MLM company will do so anyway when routinely asked by the Inland Revenue. There is no point in trying to hide anything from the inspectors, because if they get the slightest indication that you are not being fair and reasonable in your claims they are entitled to go through your complete business with a fine-toothcomb, make estimates of your income and outgoings, and charge you for estimated previously unpaid tax plus interest. If you are open with them from the start, and keep good records of your earnings and expenses, you are in the best position to be paying out the minimum possible amounts of tax. You would do well to speak to an accountant, or even your tax inspector, to find out the extent to which you can offset your expenses against tax. In order to be allowable your expenses must be wholly, necessarily and exclusively incurred in the running of the business, and could include:

- petrol used for driving to prospects' houses or to meetings of various types in furtherance of your business;
- costs of refreshments provided at your own meetings;
- products used for demonstration purposes;
- a proportion of servicing and depreciation costs of your vehicle;
- part of your telephone bill;
- business aids such as books, tapes, stationery, advertising, sales literature, tickets for seminars;
- advertising;
- bank charges;
- renewal fees;
- postage;
- costs associated with the running of your office (heating, lighting, furnishings, cleaning).

It is possible that, if you are not building your business at a particularly high speed, your business could, on paper, show an overall loss at the end of your first tax year, say 1990–91. If this is the case then you have a right, under section 381 of the Taxes Act 1988, to claim this loss from any tax paid in the 1987–88 tax year in any other employment or business. As long as the trading loss has been agreed with the inspectors, they will repay the amount with interest, as a lump sum. You can also elect to set the loss against your income in the next tax year from the same source. It is well worth the small amount of time and effort necessary to keep accurate accounts of your business, but do make sure that it *is* only a small amount of time. Later on, when your business is very profitable, you can employ an accountant to do all your work for you. Your time is precious in MLM; don't fiddle about with figures too long when you could be telephoning a prospect.

VAT

You do not need to worry about VAT, as your company will almost certainly have dealt with it in such a way as to relieve distributors of any significant administration relating to it. You can register voluntarily whatever size of business you have, but it is mandatory when your annual turnover reaches £23600 (currently). If you do register voluntarily your administration and bookkeeping will double at a stroke, and you will be subject to routine inspections.

You may save some money by being able to claim back the VAT element of your business expenses, but is it worth the trouble? You could be out building your business instead. If you are already self-employed as a sole trader, subject to VAT, when you commence your MLM business then you have no choice but to include your new business in the VAT calculations.

Budgeting

I have stated a number of times in this book that the risk of losing any significant amount of money in MLM is extremely small. However, it is quite possible to have a financial outlay (on expenses, incidentals, sales and business aids) which is totally inappropriate to the size and profitability of your business, especially in the beginning, if you have not budgeted properly. If you are not careful you may find that all your profits and more are being eaten up by these extra costs, and it is easy to become disillusioned and start to think that you may never break even. Many people have quit their business over this type of financial stress when, with a little planning and common sense, their business could have slowly and surely grown.

Your financial budgeting will depend upon what sort of MLM business you want and your personal circumstances. If you are in a steady, well-paid job when you start and you have a long-term goal of a large secure business and financial independence, it may not concern you that your new business runs at a 'loss' for some months because of your expenditure on items essential for long-term success (sales and business aids, training, travelling, seminars and conventions). At the other end of the scale, you may be in a position where immediate profitability is paramount, in which case reduction of your outlay and maximization of your income from the very start is your prime concern. Your circumstances may come somewhere between these two extremes, but the principle remains the same; you must decide what level of profitability suits you at the beginning and your expenses must be tailored to fit your decision. You might decide to plough 10, 50 or even 100 per cent of your initial profits back into your business in various forms in order to benefit in the longer term.

You should also budget for the time you expect to expend on your business. If you don't do this, two things are possible. You will spend so much time building your business that other important uses of your time (including, perhaps, family matters) will be neglected. This will eventually cause friction and be detrimental to your business and to the people around you. Alternatively, you will be distracted from building your business by the numerous other demands on your time which are not so productive, therefore removing the consistency which is so important to a thriving MLM business. When, after consultation with the relevant parties, you have decided exactly how much time you will put into the enterprise and how it will be allocated throughout each week, you can then decide how you are going to split this time into the various activities of building an MLM business: selling, sponsoring, advertising, training and motivation meetings.

Set yourself a schedule and keep to it. Your time is precious, especially when you are building an MLM business in addition to working full-time as a mother or an employee. Most people do not schedule their own time, unless their boss requires it, and they are apt to assume that no one else does and put various distractions your way. It is very easy to find yourself spending your time as others would have you spend it, rather than as you have decided to spend it. Be strict with yourself and polite and assertive with others: as Einstein discovered, 'Time is actually Money'. Don't make yourself busy with unproductive activities, but prioritise your available time so that most of it is spent on the most productive tasks. Before you retire to bed each night, make a list, in order of importance, of the tasks you must do the next day. If an extra task crops up during the day look at your list and slot it in at the appropriate place – if it helps your business to grow, it goes near the top. The tasks at the bottom of your list are those that can wait another day – non-business matters. When your business profits allow (or from the start if you can afford it), consider relieving yourself of time-consuming tasks that take away business-building time (housework, decorating, gardening) by paying for someone else to come in and do them. And how many hours a week do you watch television? How many hours do you *need* to watch it?

The following two subjects could have a significant effect upon your finances, especially at the start of your business.

Advertising Advertising in the press or on local radio can be an excellent tool for finding new customers and new distributors, if it is done properly with the correct (and legal) wording, in the right places and for a suitable length of time. However, it is a very expensive way of going about building your business, and probably requires a fairly large investment before you get it right (profitable). If you don't watch your expenditure on this item very carefully, it will eat up most, or all, of your initial profits. Wait until your profits are large enough and regular enough for you to be able to allocate a reasonable percentage to advertising. And don't forget that very big businesses have been built without any advertising!

Stockpiling 'Stockpiling' or 'inventory loading' is prohibited by some companies and ignored by others. It can sometimes seem a very attractive proposition to buy enough stock to qualify you for higher levels of discounts, although you do not actually have orders from customers and distributors which will cover the purchase. Apart from the drain on your resources, reasons for not doing this include: the risk of collapse of the company and consequent problems of refunds (admittedly a small risk, but it has happened, with the loss of many thousands of pounds of distributors' money); the negative motivation of finding buyers for the stock in order to recoup your expenditure (as in the pyramid schemes); the pointlessness of doing so – if you are so convinced that your business will develop quickly to a large turnover, you might as well wait that short period until your turnover naturally reaches the higher discount levels. The money saved by stockpiling is negligible when compared with the disadvantages of doing it.

Developing your business

Very simply, this consists of two activities: selling and sponsoring. Your business will develop to any level you choose as long as you do some of the former and as much as is necessary of the latter. These two words describe activities about which there is so much to say that a lifetime's writing would not suffice. It is only possible, within one chapter of a book, to give you the barest principles of each. Thousands of books have been written on selling, and even to recommend the best ones is difficult. On sponsoring there is a wealth of information to be had from MLM practitioners every-where, the most reliable obviously coming from the most successful distributors. 'Sponsoring' is the simple act of signing somebody into the business. You have to learn the most effective actions you can take to ensure the maximum number of new distributors signing up, and the most effective actions to take after to ensure the maximum performance of your group of distributors. This includes making a list, qualifying people, inviting people to see your business, presenting the opportunity, following up, helping new distributors get started, training, motivating, and developing the right attitudes. All this information can be gained in time by just getting out there and doing it, but experience is a slow teacher, even if it is the best one. It is far better to act on other people's experience. In the rest of this chapter and the next one you will find the basics to start you off on the right foot.

Knowledge is learning from your mistakes;
wisdom is learning from other people's mistakes.

Getting started – the list

When you start your MLM business you will have a kit which contains every ingredient necessary to make a success of your enterprise, except the one – people. This is where you come in. You have to supply people, help them to achieve their ambitions, and thus build your own profitable business. The size of your business will be directly proportional to the number of people you sponsor, and the number of people that you sponsor will be directly proportional to the number of. people to whom you show your business. You will meet a large number of people in the following months and years, and many of them will be prospects for your business because of what they have told you about their circumstances and dreams. Until you meet these people, however, you will have to make do with those you already know of. How many will that be? The answer is more than you think, and the way to find out is to make a list.

Everyone has a different perception of what 'know' means, and a list of the people you know may be much shorter than a list of the people you know *of*. The difference is important. Your list will be a prospect list, which means that those on it are future prospects for showing your business to; it does not mean that you are going to invite them to see it tomorrow. The list of people you know of will include some to whom you may never yet have spoken, but with whom you will start a conversation at some point in order to find out whether they might be interested in a business like yours. Your list will include your ex-boyfriend/girlfriend/husband/wife, the hi-fi dealer, the television repairman, the window cleaner, your children's teachers, the squash club owner, the bank cashier, your doctor, your estate agent, your plumber, your postman, shop assistants whom you see regularly, the man who walks his dog past your house every morning, the garage attendant, the librarian, the publican, your hairdresser, the trading standards officer, in fact, anyone with whom you can conceivably start a conversation. When you add these people to those you 'know' – all of your family, friends, relatives, neighbours and colleagues – and all the people that you 'have known', you will have quite a formidable list. If there are less than one hundred people on the list it is quite likely that you have not thought hard enough.

Every day, if your mind is properly attuned to the development of your business, you will meet or think of at least one more addition for your list. Keep adding them because it does not matter how long they are on it; it might take ten years before you actually manage to present your business to them. As long as you have a healthy list you will never forget anyone whom you meet for a short period, or run out of people to approach. As you work your way through your list you can cross off those whom you have confirmed are not interested and those who you have sponsored.

Qualifying people

This does not mean checking out IQs, social class, financial status, or anything of the sort. It simply means finding out whether the person you are speaking to will possibly be interested in looking at a business opportunity which could give them more money, or time, or both. The most important point of all is not to prejudge people. You do not know what people want unless you ask them. It is all too easy to look at someone and say, 'She's a wealthy company director with everything going for her. She wouldn't be interested in another business.' She might be frustrated with the long hours she has to put into the company to make it successful and could be looking for something that could give her the same income for fewer hours a week. Every person that you do not bother with because of what *you* think *they* think could be the one who will help to make you a million.

So, how do you qualify people? You can do it without them even knowing it, by bringing the conversation around to any one of a number of subjects, and asking ordinary questions about them. The obvious ones are:

- **Occupation** How long have they been in their job? Do they enjoy it? Does it pay well? Are they going to stick with it for the rest of their life?
- **Money** Are they complaining about a lack of it? What do they want that they cannot afford? Would they like a bigger house? Do they have the car they want?
- **Recreation** Where did they do for their summer holiday? Where would they like to go? What sports, hobbies, pastimes do they enjoy and can they afford the money and time to do them?
- **Family** Do they see enough of their family? Do they want private education for their children?

When you are serious about your business everyone you meet is a prospect, and they stay a prospect until you find out that they will not be interested in looking at what you have to offer. In this intervening period before you (hopefully) show them the 'plan', you have the chance to give them the (true) impression of you as an honest, considerate, positive, business-minded, goal-oriented individual. If you do this successfully your credibility with the prospect is at its highest, and your eventual invitation to them will be looked upon as a serious business proposition. This is exactly how you want it to be taken, and will give you the best possible results.

Inviting

This is the part of building an MLM business that most people find the most difficult to do, although it is *the* most important part of the business. No invitations from you to others to have a look at your business means no business for you. There are an infinite number of ways in which you can approach people with the intention of arranging to show them your business, and some are more successful for one type of MLM business than another. Similarly, some ways are best for certain people. You will have to decide which methods to use to suit you *and* your business. It may come completely naturally to you, or you may need counselling and coaxing from your sponsor. You may need to try all sorts of methods and come to find those you like the best by trial and error.

You can listen to all sorts of advice on inviting – from your sponsor, from recordings of successful distributors, from the MLM company – all of which will be excellent, but the bottom line is this: if you aren't comfortable and happy with the approaches that you use, you are not going to use them as often as you should, and therefore they are not going to give you the best possible results. Additionally, there is no single approach which is best for every set of circumstances. As you progress in your business, and develop confidence, you will begin to find it easier to say the right thing at the right time to the right people, to get the highest possible percentage of positive replies. As with every other part of the MLM business, the infallible advice is to keep on doing it and you will learn the best way to do it.

The following are some of the ways in which your business can be exposed.

Face to face

Face to face or voice to voice on the telephone is the most obvious, straightforward and effective way to invite a prospect to see your business. It is put to them openly, with a reference to a previous comment made by them which qualified them as a prospect. They will know and respect you by now and will take you seriously. What you cannot do properly is explain fully how the business works and what its advantages are for your prospect while you are standing in the street, or talking over the telephone. There is no way to get over the business's full potential unless the prospect is sitting down, giving it his full attention, and you are explaining with the aid of diagrams, literature and maybe product demonstrations. *Don't* get into too much of a detailed explanation at the invitation stage. No businessman worth his name ever tries to clinch a deal in the street. You are bound to be asked 'What is it?'. Give some sort of explanation which satisfies their curiosity; there are all sorts of ways to do this. Alternatively, speak directly about the company, its products and its business opportunity. The chances are that they will not have heard of it before. MLM is still largely unknown by the general public.

Here are some examples of ways to invite people to see the business:

'John, we've started a great new business. It may not suit you but I'd like you to take a look at it because it's extremely profitable. Will you watch this video tonight and you can tell me what you think tomorrow when I pick it up.'

'John, you know that holiday you were saying you'd like to take one day when you could afford it? Well, I might be able to help you out on that. I'm working with some people locally, building up a business. It's going to be very lucrative for the right people and we need to expand it. Would you be interested in taking a look at it?'

'John, you've been talking about having your own business at some stage, well we're looking for some partners to help us develop ours. We're helping people to start their own [company name] businesses in [products] and there's a lot of money in it if you put in the effort. I'm sure you would do well in it. Let's get together this week so I can go through it with you.'

'John, I've come across a tremendous business idea recently. It doesn't need experience or capital, the earnings potential is unlimited and you get as much free training and advice as you need. You need to see it, are you free tomorrow night?'

'John, my wife and I are associated with an international company called [name] which manufactures [products]. Along with a number of other people we have distribution rights on these products, and it's possible to make an extremely profitable business out of it. You could probably afford that holiday *this* year by putting 10–15 hours a week into it for six months. What do you think?'

'John, how many hours a week would you give me for £30000 a year?'

'John, do you want to earn what you're worth?'

'John, are you interested in making some extra income?'

'John, are you going to be doing the same job for another thirty years? How would you like to retire in five?'

'John, be round my place with your wife at eight tonight, I've got something very important to show you.'

I could go on for a hundred pages with examples like these. I am trying to put across to you that there is no ideal invitation for every occasion. Every one of the above examples will be perfect for some circumstances and not so good for others. Say what feels right at the time. It doesn't matter if it comes out all wrong, as long as you have said it; as long as you have said *anything*. If your prospect is a good one he will be 'looking' for opportunities and he will recognize yours however you say it.

Advertising

Although I have mentioned advertising above as an easy way to spend all your profits, many people use it extensively. There are usually two types of MLM advertising. One type is aimed at procuring a meeting with an interested party and the second is directed towards obtaining names and addresses of enquirers in order to send them literature about your MLM company and its opportunity. This method is usually more popular with those who would rather work primarily from home. It *is* possible to build an MLM business (I'm not sure how successfully) without venturing far from home very often. In order to do this, the products you are dealing with need to be reasonably mailable or sent in all cases direct from the company. A disadvantage of this type of MLM development is the extra costs (over and above the cost of the advertising) of the literature and the postage. Even after you have a number of interested enquirers, the response rate from the literature that you send out will be extremely low. It is also harder to encourage and motivate your downline by letter than in person, and again there are the postage costs to consider. However, the fact remains that many people like to build their business in this way, and no doubt many have been successful.

Although a press advertisement reaches a very large number of people, the disadvantage (apart from the cost) is that the readers of it do not know you. The percentage of readers who actually respond can be very, very low, so you must know what you are doing before you spend significant amounts. There are dozens of offers in the 'situations vacant', 'part-time vacancies' and 'business opportunities' columns of most papers, and some of them are quite dubious, so it is difficult to convince people that *your* offer is genuine. You can do this far better when you have established some kind of rapport and you are offering an opportunity face to face. A personal invitation is a compliment, implying that the person being approached is capable of becoming a businessman/woman.

Advertising can work if it is done right; contact your upline for advice on the best way to go about it.

Whatever kind of advertising you consider, there are numerous media through which to do it, and you will have to word your advertisement in a way that is suitable for the likely audience. Some advertising media and their advantages and disadvantages are as follows:

Local newspapers and magazines   Reasonable rates but not a very large circulation in all cases. They may be dubious about accepting your advertisement because of problems with non-genuine schemes. The advertisement is only 'live' for a week. Smaller circulation parish magazines have a life of a month or more and may be read by a higher social class (if that is important to you).

National press   Costs are out of reach for beginners in MLM, but results can be extremely good when your business can run to this level of expense. Bear in mind that you will have to be well prepared to sponsor, supply, help and motivate people who live hundreds of miles from you, so get this aspect sorted out before you consider this type of advertising. Some companies have gone in for advertising their products in the national press, referring all leads to the nearest active distributors.

Radio   An extremely large audience but the advertisement is only in existence for a few seconds. Only available (at present) on local commercial radio. Rates will vary according to the station.

Television   Prohibitively expensive and rarely (perhaps never) done. However, a large MLM company could consider TV advertising for its distributors. A few companies have advertised their products on television, passing leads to the nearest distributors.

Leaflets, posters and shop windows The lowest cost advertising, and the lowest potential audience, although the life of the advertisement is possibly the longest of all. If your advertising is going to look professional, which is recommended, there will be some extra costs of printing, or you will be able to obtain ready-made posters and small advertisements from your company. This type of advertising can be targeted with some amount of accuracy. You will have a pretty good idea of the interests of the people who will see your poster, depending on where you put it.

Business opportunity publications There are a large number of these magazines around these days, with a target audience of 'opportunity seekers'. Some of the magazines are sent out free to such people, others are distributed through a multi-level network, and others are available by subscription or straight from the newsagent. The quality of these publications ranges from dire to decent. Often advertising is free if you subscribe to the magazine. There are also nationally published advertising papers which contain 'business opportunity' columns. The disadvantage of using this type of publication is that your advertisement will be drifting in a sea of other 'opportunities' with nothing to make it stand out from the rest, unless you have spent considerable time and money on making sure that it does. In addition, unless the editors make significant efforts to ensure that only genuine opportunities appear in their magazine, your advertisement will be sitting alongside some extremely dubious and possibly illegal schemes. It is not the ideal environment for exposing your genuine and worthwhile business.

As for the wording of your advertisement, there are a million different ways to do this; take a look in some of the publications I have mentioned above. I cannot tell you what the most effective wording is, but I can tell you that any advertisement which appears week after week in the same format has got to be successful, otherwise you would not see it more than once. Use this principle as a yardstick to give you some ideas, if you feel that advertising is for you.

Tapes

Audio and video tapes can both be extremely useful business aids, and can give you the best of both worlds. You make the initial personal contact with your prospect and at the right time you give them a tape which does the inviting for you, in the words of company representatives and successful distributors. Video is most popular these days, as it can give a complete picture of the company's operation and show the faces of the speakers. All you have to do is collect the tape and arrange a time to explain the business to your prospect, assuming that he or she is interested. Apparently videos have a very high success rate, so a few of them would seem to be an essential part of your inventory. Give them out as often as possible; they are ideal for overcoming the nervousness which affects everybody when they are trying to invite others to see the business.

An extremely effective way of using a company video is to play it during a sales party. Not only do you have a captive audience, but you also have several people watching it at once, all of whom are hopefully impressed with the products already, having purchased some of them. It would probably not be effective to say to everyone in the room, 'You've all seen the products and the video, now who wants to become a distributor?', but you should certainly take full advantage of the occasion, especially as watching the video may have generated excitement in a few minds. Starting with the people who have impressed you as being positive and lively, approach as many as possible, quietly and singly, to suggest that they might like to know more about the business opportunity available.

Presenting the opportunity

This is otherwise known as 'showing the plan'. The more often you do this, the more people you will sponsor and the bigger your business will be. So, how do you show the plan? Any way you can is the answer. There are established ways, however, which have stood the test of time as the most effective methods of recruiting people. The first simple and obvious fact is that the more people you can show the business to at the same time, the more effectively you are using your time and the faster your business will grow. You need to have some meetings, the larger the better. If you are new in the business you may not feel capable of standing up in front of a group of people and talking for half an hour about a business which you have only just joined. Don't worry; your sponsor will do it for you, and if he or she can't, their sponsor will do it for you, and so on. They will all benefit from your meeting, so they will help you to make it as successful as possible. It won't be long before you will want to do the meetings yourself because you will want to explain the business *your* way.

House meetings

The best and cheapest way to get a quick start in your business is to hold some meetings at home. Book several nights with your sponsor, leaving one or two days between each one, and then get as many people as you can to your house for each of the nights. You can use any of the invitations indicated above, or any other phrases you feel happy with. You may want to advertise the meeting in such a way that any respondent is going to be definitely interested in starting up a business, although, while you still have more than a hundred names on your list, this will hardly be necessary. Perhaps the most efficient way of inviting for a meeting is to get hold of your list, pick twenty people from it, write their telephone numbers next to their names, and sit down next to the telephone. Decide what approach you are going to use and start ringing. Make your calls short and business-like. Talk about the business at the level it is; it is big, profitable and worthy of anyone's consideration, however much of a 'success' they already are. Don't describe it as 'a little part-time thing'. Have two meeting dates available so that you have the best chance of finding a suitable night for your prospects, and make sure you get a definite answer – 'Yes, I'll be there' or 'No I won't'. 'Probably' and 'I'll try' *always* means they will not come. Try it if you don't believe me. If at all possible try to get spouses and partners to the meeting as well, then you have two chances of success when you give the presentation.

Stay on the telephone until you have gone through the twenty people, and divide the number you now have by two. This is the number who are likely to turn up. When you start to build your business you will begin to realize how many people lack enough basic integrity either to keep to their word or to give you a straight answer in the first place. (One great pleasure of the MLM business is to find people of high integrity with whom you can enjoy working.) If your final number will not fill the house, make another list and go through the procedure again until you are sure of getting a good turnout.

Have some simple refreshments ready, remembering that you want the whole thing to be able to be duplicated. If you start serving alcohol at your meetings, your prospects' perception will be dulled, and others might be put off, feeling that *they* will have to incur similar expense if they get into the business. Consider displaying a polite notice asking people not to smoke, if you have any non-smokers at your meeting. The cleaner the atmosphere the more clearly the business will be understood. It is a business meeting, so make sure that it runs like one. Be efficient and punctual, and look like a successful business person. People are impressed by correct dressing, whatever they might say. What would you think if you went to hospital and were examined by someone in faded jeans and a sweatshirt? You will also need some sort of screen or display board in order to draw some diagrams of how the business works.

If you are going to give the presentation yourself there are some general points to bear in mind. You are enthusiastic (or you would not be having the meeting), so look and act as if you are enthusiastic. If you aren't, how can you expect anyone else to be? Be yourself, and talk about yourself (within reason); the people you have invited all know you and will want to know how and why you got involved in the business, to see if the same reasons might apply to themselves. Don't be afraid to use notes, as it makes the whole thing seem easy to do, and therefore duplicatable. There is no need to come over as a slick presenter, in fact, the more amateurish your presentation, the more likely your prospects will be to think that they could do the business even better than you.

Inevitably you will give a demonstration of the products involved, or at least talk about them and show them. You may want to have a display of some of the products already set up, or perhaps you will leave it until after the talking is done before you introduce them.

After some welcoming and introductory remarks, give a brief description of the concept of MLM and its advantages and opportunities, before profiling the company, its principals and its principles. Talk about the products and the market for them, and the way in which they can be sold. Then go through the details of the company's marketing plan, with suitable emphasis on the possible growth of their network and their income – if anything in the meeting is going to get people excited, this part is.

At the end of the meeting you and your sponsor can answer questions and give out literature which will help your prospects to make up their mind about becoming involved, or even sign up new distributors if you have some keen people there. Normally people will want to go home and read through some information on their own before making a decision, so you will lend them pamphlets, brochures, perhaps a video, perhaps some products. When you do this you should arrange a date and time to retrieve the items and to answer any further questions (of course with a view to signing up the person). 'Following up' is discussed later.

'Open' meetings

These are another excellent way to sponsor people, not least because of the large numbers of interested people who can be shown the business at the same time. The principle is to put across a professional image of the company and its products and opportunity by holding the meeting in a businesslike atmosphere, perhaps in a hotel conference room, with assistance from experienced distributors and perhaps also from the company. There should be a reasonable number of distributors in the area, all of whom should commit themselves to bringing at least a couple of prospects to the meeting, otherwise the whole sermon may be preached to the converted. As well as the escorted prospects at the meeting, there should be as many other people as possible, and these can be attracted by suitable advertising before the event. The team of local distributors organizing the event will of course share the cost of it, and if possible will hold identical functions every week. Attendance at the meeting should be completely free to invited guests, who should be served with light refreshments (coffee and biscuits).

The presentation should always include some detailed product information and, if at all possible, a product demonstration. Good products are the backbone of any genuine MLM scheme – in any case, those guests who don't want to take advantage of the business opportunity may be impressed enough with the products to order some before they go home! After the presentation there should be an informal period during which each guest can ask questions of their host. Literature should be freely available to all those who wish to consider the matter at length, but remember to arrange a definite time to retrieve it and answer any further queries. Any enrolments on the night will be handled by the distributor who invited the guest.

Interviewing

Another way to expose the business is by having individual interviews with invited guests and random callers at a suitable venue. It will normally require at least a small team of distributors working together in an easily accessible room or small hall. Advertising for the event should be enough to ensure a steady flow of interested people to the venue throughout the chosen day; they can have the business explained to them personally by one of the distributors present. The ideal place to hold such an event is probably somewhere in or near a shopping centre on a Saturday. This will give you the maximum possible frequency of callers.

'One-on-one'

This is MLM jargon for the situation where a distributor explains the business opportunity, with varying levels of informality, to one person. For the purpose of this book it will also mean 'one-on-two' (one distributor showing a couple), 'two-on-one' and 'two-on-two' (distributor and sponsor showing one person or a couple). Although it is perhaps not as effective a use of your time as showing the plan to a large number of people simultaneously, it is nevertheless a very good method of presentation. The advantages are the negligible amount of planning and organization (compared to a large meeting) and the chance to tailor your presentation to the particular personality and desires of your prospect. One-on-ones can be done literally anywhere – on a bus, in a café, on a park bench, in your car, in your home, in their home. It is far better to do it when the opportunity arises rather than to try to arrange a more formal occasion; by that time the prospect's interest and excitement might have evaporated. If you get the chance to show your business to anyone, anywhere, do it. The official literature and product demonstrations can come later. Many people have been sponsored after some scribbled diagrams on the back of a table napkin and a good helping of enthusiasm.

If you are going to your prospect's home you will be able to give a more professional presentation, and if your sponsor goes with you to give you some moral support because of your relative inexperience, or just to help you, the whole thing can be done even more smoothly. What you forget to say he will remember, and there will be no awkward silences. Don't rely too much upon your sponsor, though. Learn to do your own presentations as soon as you can because the principle of successful MLM is to find as many distributors as possible by showing the idea to as many people as possible. You can get through far more people by working on your own rather than waiting for someone else to fit you into their schedule.

Literature
You don't have to present your business personally, you can simply give, or send, literature that says almost everything. The only trouble with this is that it doesn't say it *all*. It will certainly not miss out important details of the marketing plan, commission structure, product benefits, and so on, as you might do, but it will lack the personal touch which is so important to sponsoring. It is possible to sign up people by giving them written information – everything works if you do it often enough – but you will not sign up as many as you would have if you had presented the opportunity personally to each of them. Remember one important fact: more often than for any other reason, people will sign up in your business because they believe in *you*. It may be quite some time before they know enough to believe in the company, and possibly even longer before they start to believe in themselves. When you are showing the plan to someone with whom you have achieved a certain empathy – you have a rapport with them and you know what they are looking for – you are far more likely to excite, motivate and strike a chord with that person, whether you are aware of it or whether it happens subconsciously. This is highly unlikely to happen between a prospect and a pamphlet.

Literature is costly. When you are lending it after a personal presentation at least you can get it back for re-use, but if you are sending it all over the country it is only ever going to be seen by one or two people. Bearing in mind the very low response rates for unsolicited mail, and the only slightly higher response rates for qualified mailshots (those following enquiries from advertising), plus the high cost of postage, expenditure on literature can be prohibitive. The final disadvantage of using literature alone for explaining your business is that the prospect is less likely to be able to see the products which form the basis of the business before making the decision whether to join up. This may not always be relevant (for example, in the case of products which are available everywhere by retail, like records), but it is a consideration for most MLM products.

What about the advantages of literature? You may not have the capability, or the desire, to spend time and effort meeting people, qualifying them, inviting them and showing them the business. You may want to run your business entirely from home, which is perfectly possible, and your only method of contacting prospects is to send out the necessary literature by post. You can reach a lot of people in a given amount of time through the post. You may have an excellent prospect for your business who lives 300 miles away so, rather than risk someone else getting her interested in some other (or the same) MLM business before you get your chance, you may decide to try to do the whole thing through the post. With a preliminary telephone call and some well-produced literature you may well find a new recruit. If you are seriously considering a 'postal' MLM business you will need to do your homework very carefully to avoid wasting substantial sums of money on 'trial and error' advertising or direct mailing. Get yourself one of the many excellent books on these subjects, learn from the wide experience of others, and do it properly.

Following up

After you have shown your prospects your MLM opportunity they will either say right away that it's not for them or they will express some interest in the business. If you are fortunate, or you give extremely good presentations, your prospects will demand to be signed up before they leave! Most people, however, need time to think about the proposition, and you should lend them enough literature and audio or video tapes to allow them to go home and study it all at their leisure. You must allow them a reasonable period to do this, but not so long that any initial excitement and interest begin to wane. If you arrived at their house at the agreed time and find the borrowed information lying on the doorstep, you will know that you do not need to waste any more time with them. Did you want that kind of person in your business anyway?

If someone is willing to talk to you about what they have seen, they are interested. The more questions they ask, the more interested they are, so make sure that you have all the answers ready. If you don't know them all, take your sponsor with you.

A prospect may initially say 'no' to the business, but 'no' can often mean 'I need more information', or 'try harder'. If they say they don't want to join up, or can't join up, don't say 'why not?', or you will get them on the defensive straight away. Just keep listening and they will continue to explain themselves while you are taking it all in and preparing your responses. Remember this: before you showed them the business you qualified them. You found out that they were looking for something that more money could help them find. You offered to show them a way to find what they were looking for, and they came to see what you had. When you are following up with them you *know* that they need the business. You know what their dream is and you can hold it up in front of them. Their negative reactions may be based on fear of success, a lack of self-confidence bred by years of discouragement which convinces people that they cannot be successful in anything. Your belief in their capability for the task may be difficult for them to accept, and they need you to convince them that they can do it. So keep listening. When they have given you a reason say, 'Is that the only reason?' If it isn't, wait for the next one. When you have the reasons, you can answer them with empathy, perhaps using the 'feel, felt, found' method – 'I know how you feel, I felt the same way, but let me tell you what I found out . . .'

When you have found out all their objections and answered them, they may use another delaying tactic: 'I can't start it until . . .' You could then suggest that an excellent way of starting the business is to sign up now and start getting used to the products, so that when they are ready to start building their own business they will be fully conversant with the products and more confident in selling them.

There are certain common objections put forward by prospects to explain why they cannot join the business. What are the answers to them?

'I don't have the time.'

This must rank as the most popular objection. Time is the one thing, the only thing, of which we all have exactly the same amount in a day, down to the last microsecond. The only possible thing that this objection can mean, whenever it is said, is 'I am not putting that activity very high on my list of priorities.' Think back to the reason why they came to see the business; making more money *was* high on their list of priorities. Refer to this and remind them how they can multiply their time by building a group, and in the long run have more free time than they have ever had before. The business can be developed in just ten effective hours per week. How much time do they spend watching television? Some of the most successful distributors in MLM were extremely busy people when they started, but they had the vision to see that if they made themselves even busier for a limited period of time they would reap the reward of a lifetime of more money, and more free time than they ever had in which to spend it. Not having much time is a reason for doing the business, not a reason for *not* doing it. Offer to take them to the next meeting where they can talk to some distributors who were even busier than them when they started, and who will explain how they overcame their time challenges.

'I couldn't sell anything.'

When was the last time they went to see a great film at the cinema? Did they keep it to themselves when they came home? Of course not; they told everyone who would listen what a great film it was, and their enthusiasm probably encouraged half a dozen people to go and see it. What's the difference if you substitute great products for the great film? There's no difference. If they use the products themselves and like them, they will talk about them and consequently they will gain custom. Once they start building a group, the selling takes care of itself as the group start using and enthusing about the products.

'I don't think I could do it.'

This really means, 'I would really love to do it, but I'm scared.' They need your encouragement and help, they need to know that you will hold their hand while they take their first steps into the adventure of a lifetime. You could answer, 'With my help I know you could find six people who *could* do it.'

Remember when you are following up that you can't talk people into the business, but you can *listen* them into it.

If you gain a new distributor after you follow-up you can take them straight back to the beginning of this chapter and get them started. If it is clear that they are not going to join you, ask them if they would like to try the products, if they are not already a customer. More often than not you will turn your prospect into a new customer. Before you leave you have one more opportunity to make your time with this person worthwhile. Try to get a referral from them: 'Debbie, I appreciate that the business is not for you, but you've seen what a good opportunity it would be for the right person. Do you know of anyone who would be interested in making some extra income?' Some of the wealthiest distributors were found by being referred by someone else.

Summary points

1. 'Success' is achieving *your* goals. Don't let others impose their goals upon you, and don't impose yours on them.
2. You are running a business, so treat it like one. Don't forget the Inland Revenue, and plough some of your profits back into your business.
3. Make that list! Use it and add to it daily.
4. Develop your own approaches and dump those you don't like.
5. Qualification, invitation, presentation, follow-up, ask for referrals – in that order, and as often as possible.

6: The Basics of Successful Selling

This chapter will tell you about:

- where to get the best advertising;
- the most profitable form of selling;
- selling without even trying;
- where to find customers.

These subjects deserve a chapter of their own because of the overriding importance of selling in MLM. Absolutely nothing happens, in any business, until something is sold. All business involves selling goods or services of one kind or another. I make no claim to give you everything you will ever need to know to be a great salesman; there are thousands of books on this subject, and you should buy one of these if you want to learn more. This section covers the *basics* of successful selling.

Sharing, not selling

A salesperson working for a large corporation would probably be given an area to work in and targets to meet. MLM could not be more different. You can sell as much or as little as you like, where you like, when you like, to whom you like. The only person who should give you targets is you. Selling *is* important in MLM, but this should not put you off getting involved or provide an excuse for not participating, because MLM selling does not have to be 'selling' in the accepted sense of the word. Direct selling is in a class of its own; it is basically friends doing business with friends. No pressure or hard sell is necessary. There's nothing to stop you selling in any way you like, but MLM is all about a *lot* of people selling a *little*, as opposed to a few people selling a lot in the conventional company set-up. You may class yourself as some kind of super salesperson, and that's fine – if you can build yourself a group of like-minded people, you will need far fewer to reach the top levels than the novice with his or her group of novices (but there are more novices around than experts and they are therefore easier to recruit. No one need have any fears about whether they have enough selling skills when they are thinking about coming into MLM, because skills are just not necessary.

So, how do you sell? Remember that in MLM you need only sell a small amount, as long as you can duplicate your efforts. If you have chosen your company well and picked one with products that you like and would buy yourself, you are halfway to being able to sell them. All you need to do now is use them, enjoy them and decide for yourself what the benefits of using them are. When you have done this you will, or should, have the one essential quality that will ensure your sales success; enthusiasm. Enthusiasm about the products will sell them, it's that simple. You will want to tell everyone how good they are and what benefits they have given you, and by doing so you will be selling without even knowing it. In other words, as they say in MLM circles, you will be 'sharing' the products, not selling them.

Let me give you some examples. Ms C has never considered herself to be a saleswoman, but uses many of the products of the MLM company of which she is a distributor. One of her friends was telling her how, when her drains were being unblocked, large deposits of white gunge were found to be the cause. Without even thinking, Ms C said, 'It may be your washing powder. I use XYZ which is highly concentrated and doesn't have any fillers in it, and I have never had a blocked drain.' She shared her experiences of the product, and her friend ordered some on the spot. Ms J carries her box of perfume samples around with her wherever she goes. She doesn't have to say anything, people come up to her and ask her what's in it. She flips it open, lets them have a smell, and invariably gets a sale. Mr P has lost 10kg of unwanted weight by using ABC's meal replacement drinks twice a day. Everywhere he goes people ask him how he lost weight and he of course has to tell them about ABC's wonderful product. Every time he takes one of his drinks he lets someone taste it and tells them what ABC has done for him.

Does he sell much ABC? You bet he does. Share your products with people and they will share their money with you.

You can see how easy selling is, and how little of it has to be done to make your MLM business work. But think how much bigger your business could be if you were able to sell twice as much and inspire your group to do the same. Wouldn't it be worth your while to learn some of those principles of selling that would help you double the size of your business? If you read on you will find some useful and profitable information with which to embellish your selling abilities.

Product knowledge

Before you start approaching customers with your products you must know something about them. The more you know about your products and the benefits of them the more you will sell. The best way to learn about them is to use them and read everything you can about them. Not only do you learn by experience by using your products, but you also demonstrate your belief in them to everyone who sees you using them, and if you have picked the right company with the right products for you, your enthusiasm will begin to develop. Genuine belief and enthusiasm sell far more effectively then any planned sales patter. The more you know about the products the more questions you will be able to answer about them, the more objections you will be able to overcome, and the more you will be able to point out the benefits your products have over the competition. Don't make the mistake of trying always to give an answer to a query even if you aren't sure about it; if you give the wrong one your credibility with the customer will go down rapidly. If you don't know the answer say, 'I'll find out about that and get back to you.'

Planning

Just as the other part of your MLM business (sponsoring) needs planning beforehand, so does your selling if your time is to be used to its best advantage. You should decide what level of sales you intend to make per week in addition to your sponsoring activities in order to obtain the income you desire. A good level of sales from the start of your business can provide you with a significant income immediately, whereas the income from wholesaling and royalties will take a little time to develop. When you have a group volume which puts you at the highest discount level, retailing becomes very lucrative because you will be keeping all of the discount. Make some goals for the retail side of your business, and split them into manageable periods so that you know how much time you are going to spend every day or every week on developing your retail business. Purchase some customer record cards (your company is sure to have them available) to keep personal details and purchases. Have a basic stock of products for demonstrating and supplying immediately. When a customer wants your goods he wants them now, and you are giving him a better service if you can supply him now.

Finding customers

There are all sorts of ways of finding customers for your products, and the best ways for you will depend on the type of products you are selling and the type of person you are. If you are selling perfumes you could stroll into a High Street shop, open your sample case, let the staff smell them, and take orders. Your company may supply a glossy brochure which you can take around door to door, leave with people, going back later to collect any orders. Your products might be more suited to person-to-person demonstration. Whatever method suits the products must also suit you, but however they are going to be sold you need to make some preparations.

You need to make a list! (If you plan a big business, you will already have done this in the way described earlier.) It is up to you whether you go through your list showing people the business first or the products first, the important thing is to go through it at all, and to add names to it continually. If you want to develop some retail customers from scratch you will probably have to make some appointments to show people your range of goods. Start with the people you know well – family, friends, neighbours – people who are not going to refuse your request to show them your wares. This will give you the confidence to move on to other acquaintances who do not know you so well. List the people you are going to contact (the telephone is invariably the most efficient method), put a smile on your face (they will not see it but it will make a difference to how you sound), and call them. There is no need for a script, just be your own enthusiastic self and tell your story. It might go something like this:

'Hi Mary, how are you? Hey, guess what, we've gone into business! John and I have become distributors of XYZ products, they're really top quality and the range is fantastic. I know you'll like them. Can I come round for half an hour one day this week and show you what we've got?'

If you are showing people the business first, the ones that are not interested are prime prospects for customers. They will probably be only too pleased to be able to respond positively to you on something.

Telling, not selling

Talk about your products to everybody; you're proud of them, so let everyone know what you sell. More important than talking, however, is listening; you have two ears and one mouth! If you listen carefully to what people are saying you will find that they frequently give you reasons why they should be using your products. Pick up on these signals and, with the comprehensive knowledge you have about the benefits of your products, you will be able to introduce them regularly to new people. Don't forget that every customer is also a potential distributor!

Get attention from people by asking them a question they have to answer positively:

'How would you like to cut your food bills and get healthier at the same time?'
'Would you like to know how you can get water from your tap at 1p a litre that tastes just as good as that bottled stuff you buy at 40p a litre?'
'What perfume would you buy if money was no object?'
'Do you want to save time and money on doing your laundry?'

Give people a reason to talk to you about your products. Depending on the type of product, you could take some of them with you whenever you go out. People are naturally inquisitive and will want to know all about them. Some companies supply badges for their distributors to wear; it sounds a bit daft, but it works! Will the likelihood of increased profits help you rise above the slight embarrassment you might feel wearing a badge that says 'Lose weight now – ask me how!'? Distributors who wear these badges *always* get a chance to talk about their products when they go out.

Doing business with businesses

Although direct selling is generally thought of as selling to people in their homes, there are no rules that say you cannot go further afield in your prospecting for custom. Think of other outlets for your goods; whom do you do business with on a regular basis? Why shouldn't they do business with you? What other businesses might need your goods? Although they may have to be given a special discount, business customers can be extremely good customers, getting through many times more product than an individual. Launderettes use a lot of washing powder; health clubs sell a lot of meal replacement drinks and vitamins. However, don't make the costly mistake that a friend of mine once did. In his eagerness to obtain a large regular order from a business customer, he discounted the price to a level which meant that, after taking into account travelling expenses, time and extra stock needed for immediate delivery, he made a loss on every item!

Parties

Parties can make you more commission per hour than almost any other form of selling, and they can also represent the most enjoyable method of selling. If your goods are suitable for the party-plan approach you should certainly consider this form of retailing. Your company will supply ready-made invitations and probably some helpful guidelines on preparing and giving a sales party. They should also make available to you, at low cost, a good range of gifts for party hostesses. If managed correctly, your first party could be the start of a permanent series, each party being held by a guest of the previous one. Again, your company, or at least your upline, should provide all the assistance you need to make sure your parties are successful and that at least one further party is booked at every one you hold.

Going public

What regular public events are held in your locality? Shows, exhibitions, fêtes, bazaars and so on are excellent venues for exposing your products (and your business) if you do it right. The whole thing can be costly and tiring, so share the effort and the expense with other distributors, ideally your own group for maximum profitability. Make sure you book your pitch well in advance to get a good position with the maximum pedestrian traffic. It's a waste of time and effort to create a wonderful display if you end up stuck in a corner.

A lot of preparation will be necessary in order to create an attractive and professional-looking stand. You will have to obtain a good amount of stock to exhibit and create a crowd-pulling display, and this is where working as a group will be essential. Although your company is likely to have rules about what can and can't be done with the products at a public event (for example, you may be allowed to take orders but not to make any sales on the day), they should back your initiative and at the very least give you some assistance by supplying advertising materials, posters, display goods and possibly even some staff commitment. Ask them!

Advertising

This is much more expensive than talking. It gets in front of many more people than you ever can by yourself, but it doesn't give a personal touch in the way that you can. Like every other way of finding customers, it can be very effective if done properly. Advertising in the press can easily seem attractive to someone new to MLM because it means that you avoid the 'frightening' task of contacting people directly. However, think carefully before you start spending money on press advertising. Advertising costs can eat up your profits faster than anything else if you are not in perfect control of your finances. Do not start it unless you can afford to throw that amount of money down the drain without worrying about it.

Advertising can take many forms, and doesn't always have to be a small ad in the local paper. Your company will undoubtedly supply flyers and pamphlets relating the benefits of your products, and these can be distributed everywhere and anywhere – newsagents' noticeboards, doctors' waiting-rooms, stations, local shops, clubs, pubs, and so on. Why not send one back with any bills you pay? The clerk whose job it is to open your letter will probably be far more interested in your literature than in yet another cheque. Local people are far easier to supply that those further afield, so think how can you get your message cross to them? Does the parish magazine carry advertisements? Are your pamphlets suitable for dropping through letterboxes locally?

Some companies will advertise nationally and pass 'leads' on to the nearest distributor – does yours? If not, will it contribute to a sustained advertising campaign organized by a group of distributors? If the cost can be split in this way, the advertising can be larger, more eye-catching, more frequent and much more effective for all concerned.

Referrals

You should never forget referrals as a way of finding more customers. Whether you have made a sale or not, whenever you leave a person always ask if they know anyone who would benefit by using your products. If they like the products they will be only too pleased to recommend someone else for them, and they may even do the job for you. If they did not become a customer, they will probably feel better about it if they can at least help you out in this way.

Customer care

What could be better for your business than having loyal customers who buy from you again and again and again. They are the foundation of any solid business. They reduce the need for continually seeking new customers, and they are the best form of advertising you can have. Of course you should never stop looking for new customers, but you must also make sure that you never neglect your existing ones. Put a label with your name and telephone number on every product and see how easy it is to sell when your customers telephone *you* for their products. The beauty of direct selling is that you give customers the personal service that they cannot get from a shop. No one wants to go traipsing around the shops for a regular purchase when they can pick up the telephone and have it delivered. It takes a while to train customers to this level of appreciation of your service, but it is well worth the trouble.

Caring for your customers means giving them the kind of service, pleasantness, promptness and reliability that makes them glad to receive your calls and visits. It means not always talking about yourself, but allowing them to talk about themselves. It means always having in stock one each of whatever the customer usually orders so that you can deliver it as soon as they want it. It means turning up when you say you will, smiling and looking smart. It means exchanging goods and giving refunds without question. It means remembering their birthday, sending them a Christmas card, and knowing the names of their family members. It means giving them a free sample of something occasionally, as a 'thank you'. It means listening to them more than you talk to them, finding out their needs and trying to provide a product that will meet those needs. And it means saying 'thank you', and meaning it, when you leave them.

If you care for your customers you will have them for a long time. You will be able to introduce to them your complete range of products in due course, without any pressure, merely by showing them a new item every so often and leaving them one of your demonstration items to use for a few days. In this way you will be able to maximize sales to each customer, a very efficient way of increasing your business volume.

Credit

Don't give it. You are not doing your customers any favours at all by letting them pay you some time after delivery of the goods. The type of people who ask for this service are usually the type that forget to pay you when they say they will. This leads to extra work for you, the customer feeling hounded, and eventually resentment on both sides. Giving credit also upsets your cash flow and makes it harder to account for income and expenditure properly. (These comments do not apply to credit card sales, which some companies offer; these are as good as cash to you.)

The customer is always right

A cliché, but true. Never get into any kind of argument with your customer; you may win the argument but lose the customer. Do not talk about contentious matters or get too deeply involved in conversations about current affairs, politics, religion, and so on; you could easily rub them up the wrong way without even realizing it. Remember that you are there to sell your goods in the most efficient and friendly way possible.

Summary points

1. MLM is about a lot of people selling a little.
2. Knowledge and enthusiasm does the selling.
3. Have a party.
4. Talk about your products, everywhere you go.
5. Get a referral.
6. Satisfied customers are the best, and the cheapest, advertising you can get.

7:   Principles of Success

Here are twenty-three principles to put you on the road to riches in MLM:

- Persistence
- Consistency
- Commitment
- Desire
- Exposure
- Goal-setting
- Solid foundations
- Positive attitude
- Self-image
- Enthusiasm
- Immediacy
- Big thinking
- Being yourself
- Professionalism
- Motivation
- Inspiration
- Association
- Education
- Delegation
- Communication
- Recognition
- Integrity
- Auto-suggestion

Persistence

This principle is first because it is the most important of all. If you totally ignore every other piece of advice you get from this book and elsewhere, you will still succeed in MLM, and probably at anything else in life, if you will just apply this one principle.

In every survey of how people have made fortunes from humble beginnings, persistence is the recurring theme. They never give up. However many failures they have, they pick themselves up, dust themselves off, figure out where they went wrong, and try again. Success always seems to come just after the biggest failure of all, the one that convinces most people that it just isn't worth carrying on with the venture. You have an advantage in MLM; you cannot have a big failure and you cannot go bankrupt. The worst that can happen is *nothing*.

While building up your business you will suffer all sorts of disappointments and frustrations, mainly with people. People who promise to come to your house for a meeting will not turn up. People who pretend that they are really interested in starting a business with you will be out when you turn up at their house to sign them up. You will sponsor someone who you are convinced will blaze a trail for your business, only to see them quit after a few weeks. You will lose good people for all sorts of reasons, and you may get to the stage where you think that it just is not going to work for you. Keep going and it will; it has to. It is impossible not to get where you want to go if you will only keep going. Every major achievement in the world is due to persistence. It does not matter how fast you go forward as long as you are always advancing.

In MLM you are looking for a minimum of five people like you. People who are looking for more in their life: more money, more time, more fun. You are surely not conceited enough to think that you are the only person around with such desires. You *know* there are others like you who can see the attractions of a good MLM business and are willing to put some effort into making such a business work for them. They *are* there, waiting for someone like you to come along and give them an opportunity to change their life to how they want it. All you have to do is find them. Well, it's possible that the first ten people you speak to will sign up and build themselves, and you, a successful business. The chances of this happening, however, are infinitesimal. The laws of probability will ensure that your six dynamic distributors are carefully scattered throughout the population so that your task in finding them is just as difficult as it is for everyone else. The difficult part is that the people who want your business are very cleverly disguised as normal people. They look exactly like everyone else, with no outward indication that they are the ones you want. You have to talk to them to find out! And then there's another snag – sometimes they don't even know themselves whether they are the right ones for your business. You have to go through the same procedure with every person – qualifying, inviting, explaining and following up, and only after all that will you both know whether your prospect is for the business. And even then some will change their mind later!

You may have to approach one hundred people in order to get thirty to see your business. Of that thirty you may be lucky enough to sign up ten into your business. And out of that ten you may find that only one has got what it takes to make a success of it. So if you are looking for six good people you may have to approach six hundred. It sounds like a lot of people, doesn't it, but it would take you less than two years of approaching one person a day. Is that too big a price to pay for the prize of an expanding, highly profitable business? You could spend every day of the year showing your business to people, and have 364 refusals (unlikely), but what if the 365th person became the most successful distributor ever? Suppose this happened every year for six years – you would have a gigantic business with money rolling in fast. How many businesses can say that after six years? Wouldn't it have been worth all the effort?

In MLM you have the great advantage of knowing that the people you are looking for *are* there. The only foolproof way of reaching them is by persisting in showing your business to people. Let me put it another way. If you saw someone drop a diamond worth a million pounds into an eight-wheeled lorry being loaded with 30 cubic metres of sand and ballast, and you were given the chance to retrieve that diamond for yourself, how long would you spend looking for it? A day? A week? A month? You would spend as long at it takes to find it, because you *know* it is there.

Neither of my two young daughters could walk at one year old, but soon after they started to try. We would hold them up and set them off. First they would collapse after one step every day for a fortnight, perhaps. Then they would manage maybe two steps before the inevitable fall. After fifty attempts at walking three steps they still did not give up trying. They, like every other child, did not recognize failure except as one step on the way to success. They persisted until they succeeded.

Failure is a guaranteed ingredient of success. The most successful businessmen are in that position because they made more mistakes than everybody else. The difference between them and everybody else is that they were able to learn from those mistakes, and applied that knowledge at their next attempt. In his classic book *Think and Grow Rich*, Napoleon Hill proclaims:

'Every adversity, every failure and every heartache carries with it the seed of an equivalent or a greater benefit.'

And somebody else once said that 'Success is 1 per cent inspiration and 99 per cent perspiration.'

Whatever happens to you in the course of your MLM business, you *will* succeed if you keep going. Quitters never win – winners never quit.

Winston Churchill has the last word on this subject here, even though this story has been told innumerable times. In his second term of office he addressed a graduation ceremony. He rose to the podium, looked into the eyes of the young men and women who were about to start out in their lives, and delivered one of the shortest and most effective speeches that has ever been given:

'Never . . . give up.'

A full thirty seconds of silence reigned while he let the audience absorb the importance of his words. Then he continued:

'Never . . . give up.'

Once again, there was utter silence as the great leader continued to stare at the assembled graduates. Another minute went by and Churchill spoke his final sentence:

'NEVER . . . give up.'

Consistency

A close ally of persistence, consistency is an essential quality for MLM success. I have already said that this type of business is usually developed on a part-time basis, but what is part-time? To some it will be twenty-five hours a week, to others it will be five. It does not matter how much time a week you spend working on your business, you will make it eventually, but only if you are *consistent*. Consistency means that your hours are the same each week, perhaps increasing on occasions, but never decreasing. You are going to get nowhere by being a sponsoring superman one week and a TV addict the next. You have to work steadily towards your goals. Remember the story of the hare and the tortoise? There is a lot of truth in it. When you build up a small group they will be watching you for inspiration and example. You need to show them how to be consistent with their business.

I wrote this book over a period of six months, spending three to four hours a night on it, **consistently**. While I did this the writing flowed. As I started each night I was able to carry on from where I had left off, as if I had never stopped. My current thoughts did not have time to evaporate away as they were put back into action after only twenty hours. On a couple of occasions, however, social activities took me away from the book for several days. These were welcome breaks but it was extremely hard to get back into the flow of my subject because of the seepage of thoughts and ideas over the period of rest.

This is what happens with your MLM business if you are not consistent. Consistency builds momentum, keeps your business on track, and keeps you alert and up to date with what your business is doing and what you need it to be doing. Think of your business as a large flywheel on well-oiled bearings. Once you have built up speed you have a lot of momentum, and you need apply only a small amount of regular energy to it to keep the speed constant. Leave it to itself for a day or two and its speed will dramatically decrease, a little longer and it will stop altogether. In either case the energy required to bring back the best speed of the flywheel is greater than the amount needed daily to keep it going. Your business is no different. Do *something* every day. If every hour of effort is carefully planned for maximum effectiveness, so much the better, but if not, you must still get something achieved every day.

A very wealthy couple of American distributors once said at a rally: 'It never seemed as if we did an awful lot, but we did something every day.'

Commitment

If you start an MLM business with the statement, 'I'll give it a try and see if it works,' it won't. If you say, 'I'll see what happens,' you'll see nothing. This is true for all business ventures and many other things in life. Nothing happens until you get up, get going and make it happen.

Suppose you have shown your MLM business to a dynamic couple who seem to have everything going for them – they know everyone in town, they are highly motivated, well-respected and popular, they have potential like you've never seen, they seem to be absolutely the ideal couple to shoot to the top of the business. You sponsor them with great excitement and you can't wait to see what they do with the business. Several months later, to your great dismay, you find that they do precisely nothing with it. This type of experience can knock you so hard that you begin to doubt whether the whole thing is possible at all. After all, if a couple like that don't do anything with the business, who will? This scenario illustrates an important principle which can be nicely summarized in the following equation:

$$\text{Potential} - \text{Commitment} = \text{Nothing}$$

How is commitment achieved? It starts with the realization of the possibilities of the business you have begun. This will come through knowledge of the subject and association with people who have reached the levels to which you aspire. Perception of the potential of the business, allied to a strong desire to have the rewards that are offered through it, should bring you to the threshold of commitment. This can be put in the form of another equation:

$$\text{'I } can \text{ do it'} + \text{'I } must \text{ do it'} = \text{'I } WILL \text{ do it'}$$

The wonderful thing about the human mind is that when it is firmly told (not asked) that a certain job has to be done by a certain time, it stops finding excuses and reasons why the job can't be done or is difficult to do, and just gets on and does it. When you commit yourself to a task you get it done. Getting committed is the hard part. Usually in life, especially in a job, the motivation comes from outside – you have to get that task done properly or you are out of a job – and is negative. Someone else sets your targets for you and, in reaching them, you assist them to reach theirs. Setting your own targets is more difficult, and reaching them requires a great deal of positive motivation. Nobody is going to jump on your back if you don't reach your own goals in your own business, and the only person you are going to let down is you. It can help if you make a definite gesture of commitment, like telling several people what your goals are and asking them to monitor your progress, so that you make sure that you don't let them see you fail.

I personally experienced the power of commitment in my pastime of running. My running partner, a neighbour, is an annual half-marathon runner, and for three consecutive years I was inspired to run the Robin Hood half-marathon with him. The race is at the end of September, so in June we would start talking about whether we were going to participate. When we had decided to take part the training began, and our usual four-mile runs became longer and longer. The trouble was that if there was the slightest temptation to cut down the distance or miss out one of the three runs of the week, I would succumb to it because I knew that I could always back out at any time without any penalty. If I did do the planned training run I would be moaning to myself about the time it was taking or how tired I was feeling that evening. At that point I was not committed to the task.

When August arrived, we realized that if we did not send off the registration fee we would not be in the race at all. I sent off my six pounds, unaware that this was my act of commitment. Whether it was a morbid fear of wasting six pounds or the signature I put on the application form, I was now committed to running the race in a reasonable time, and from that moment I never missed a training run or made any more excuses. My only thought was 'I am going to run a half-marathon in September and this is what I need to do in order to make it.' There was no question of not finishing the race; it was going to be done and I was doing what was necessary to get it done.

When you become committed in your MLM business, you will no longer question whether it is going to work for you, whether you are cut out for this type of business, whether you have picked the right company, and so on. You will simply get the job done, however, long it takes, knowing that the achievement of your goal is a foregone conclusion.

I have heard people say, 'I'm going to give it everything I've got.' That sounds like commitment, doesn't it? Sometimes, however, everything you've got is not enough, and you have to commit yourself to giving even more than you think you've got in order to get where you want to be. True commitment is when you say, 'I'm going to do whatever it takes.'

Building a big MLM business can be really hard work. You may become disheartened, disappointed with people, frustrated, tired, and ready to quit. But wait – this is also true of your full-time job, isn't it? You crawl out of bed every day, and spend eight hours getting disheartened, frustrated and tired so that *someone else* can achieve their dreams. You will do whatever it takes to get that salary cheque at the end of the month and avoid getting sacked. Why not commit yourself to doing whatever it takes to make *your* dreams come true?

Once they have joined one company and had mediocre results, many people are tempted to see if the grass looks greener with another company. If you are not doing much with the business you've got, probably every other company's marketing plan looks more attractive. Commitment means sticking to a decision once you have made it, assuming you made it for the right reasons and no substantial changes have occurred since you made it. If you will not do what it takes to build a business with one company you are unlikely to do what it takes with another company. So make the right choice at the beginning – you have much of the information you will need in your hands right now – and trust your decision. Don't spend time worrying about whether your decision was the right one because your business seems to be taking too long to grow. If you do what is necessary you will succeed, whatever company you are with. All the plans work, if you work them.

If you are shown another business while you are busy building the one you chose, take a very careful look at it (it is important to increase your knowledge of the subject, in any case). Think back to the reasons why you chose the company you are with and compare those aspects with what is on offer from the new company, disregarding the hype that may be surrounding it. How big have you built the original business? Is it worth starting from scratch again (it is by no means certain that your group will follow you into the new company's scheme)? Can you afford to lose a certain amount of credibility? Confirm or reject your previous decision on a basis of fact and logic. However, if you find yourself changing companies two or more times, the problem is likely to be with you, not with the companies.

Another common activity among people 'into' MLM is to sign up for a number of schemes simultaneously in the belief that profitability will be higher. This may be quite fun to do, but isn't it a bit confusing? Which one will you show your new prospect? Will you show them all the opportunities at once? What about all the paperwork? If you want to run several businesses at the same time it's up to you, but I have never heard of a distributor who became rich by building four businesses at the same time.

Desire

I make no apology for being inspired by Napoleon Hill's writings on this subject in his book *Think and Grow Rich*. His is probably the clearest and most concise exposition of the power of desire ever written.

I have already said that if there is one quality that you should have above all others in order to be successful at MLM or any other endeavour, it is persistence. What is it that makes people persist? It is all very well to say that persistence pays off every time, but there must be a reason for it. That's easy, you say, the reason is 'more money', but you know as well as I do how few people who say they want more money actually go out and do what is necessary to get it. Something much more than a mere 'want' is required before you can overcome every adversity that comes your way, no matter what it is, and continue to strive forward and be absolutely certain of reaching a goal. What is required is nothing less than a *burning desire*. This 'must have' attitude is also necessary before you are able to make a true commitment (*see* pages 114–16).

I am not trying to suggest that, if you are looking for an extra thirty pounds a week out of your MLM business, you are not going to make it unless you feel like your life depends on it. I am talking here about the heights of success and wealth in this business. Before you reach these levels you must have a burning desire for riches. It may not happen straight away, it could creep up on you without you realizing, but you cannot produce it 'on demand'. You either have it now, or you acquire it through the realization that you can have anything you want in MLM (and in life, of course) if you are willing to pay the price for it. You will recognize your burning desire when you start to say things like, 'I just can't live without one of those air-conditioned Mercedes for much longer', 'I've *got* to have a swimming pool in the garden, I've just got to', 'That is *definitely* the last time I am travelling second class on a plane; it's first class or nothing from now on', or, perhaps the most likely of all, 'I've had enough of that job. I'm going to be my own boss if it kills me.'

Once you get your burning desire, persistence and commitment will come naturally to you. No more will you complain that 'this is hard work', wonder 'is this ever going to work?', or say 'I'm not doing anything tonight, I'm too tired'. The certain knowledge that your all-consuming needs will be met will allow you to disregard these matters as minor irritations on the journey to your goals. Anything is possible if the desire to achieve it is strong enough.

This section ends with a quotation (Napoleon Hill again) which puts everything you have just read into a powerful statement of truth:

> Anybody can wish for riches, and most people do, but only a few know that a definite plan, plus a burning desire for wealth, is the only dependable means of accumulating wealth.

Exposure

Many people new to MLM forget, in the excitement and apprehension of the initial stages of their business, some of the basic facts behind the concept. It is essential to keep these in the forefront of your mind if the business is to be successful. They are:

1. There are many thousands of people out there who want to get into your business.
2. They are all mixed in with the people who do not want the business.
3. The only way to find the people who want it is to show them the business.

4. The more people you show the business to, the more of that percentage of the population who want it you will find.

MLM is a game of numbers. There *is* a definite percentage of the popultion who would want a business like the one you can offer them. It is impossible to know just what this figure is, but it is a definite figure. It may be one in twenty, one in fifty, or one in the hundred, but whatever it is, the faster you get through the numbers the faster you will find the ones you want.

Exposure, then, should be one of the key words for your business. If you are going to spend a day plucking up the courage to approach a good prospect, then three hours showing her the opportunity, and another two hours following up later, then your business is going to grow really slowly. Not only that, but if you have spent this much time showing the thing to one person, how can you promote it as a part-time business?

For a business as large as possible, as fast as possible, it must be shown to every possible prospect at every possible opportunity. Be ready to explain your business in fifteen minutes, any time, anywhere. Carry suitable literature with you wherever you go – carry your products if possible. Use every business aid supplied by your company. Professionally-produced audio and video tapes giving a comprehensive picture of the company are usually available and can save you many hours a day. While you spend an hour on the telephone going through your list, six video tapes could be showing the opportunity to twelve or more people simultaneously. Always collect them after twenty-four hours because:

- you want them for someone else the next day;
- you can get a commitment from the person to watch it within a certain period;
- if they like the idea you catch them at the peak of interest.

Nothing is more effective than a face-to-face discussion about the business with a prospect, but if this cannot be easily arranged use your literature. Send a covering letter saying, in your own words, how excited you are about your new venture and why you feel the person would benefit from the business themselves. Tell them you will contact them when they have had a chance to read through the information, and make sure you do so.

Talk, talk, talk, talk, talk, to anyone and everyone. It doesn't matter what about. You will soon get your chance to bring in some mention of your business. If you don't, and you have established any kind of rapport with the person, you can always try to get enough information to locate them in the future. Virtually everybody is interested in making more money, more time, or more out of life – how many individuals do you know of who are totally contented with what they have? Expose your business to *everyone*; the person you omit might have been the one who would have reached for the stars and helped to make you both rich.

Meetings, the bigger the better, are an excellent way of exposing your business because you are duplicating your time. If you can take five people to a big meeting one evening, you have saved yourself two evenings (the time it would have taken to show four of them the business consecutively). If you can set up your own meeting and get a dozen prospects to come, you can multiply your time twelvefold. Best of all, when you have developed a reasonably-sized group, hold a large meeting where you and all of your group each bring a number of prospects. Now you have multiplied the effectiveness of your time twenty-, thirty-, even fiftyfold.

Whenever you are planning to show your business, think first, 'Is this the most effective use of my time?' Could you be showing it to someone else at the same time? Has your prospect any friends who would like to come and sit in while you explain it? Would your prospect mind if you brought someone else along? Is there anyone whom you could call on after, or before, your visit, to make your journey twice as worthwhile? Who could you leave a copy of your company's video with while you go out to show the plan? Have you taken some literature with you in case you get the chance to give it to someone on the way? If you are going to explain the business to someone in a public place, make sure you can be seen and heard by the people around you – it can have dramatic effects on eavesdroppers!

Rallies, seminars, training sessions and similar functions are fun, motivating, and an essential part of building your business, *but* the time and effort spent on these functions must be carefully weighed against what else you could be doing with that time. Do not cut these events out of your business entirely, because you will miss out on a lot of information, inspiration and association with successful people, all of which can do wonders for your business. Just keep them in perspective. It is quite common for distributors to enjoy the motivation and excitement of the functions so much that they neglect their business to such an extent that it stops, or doesn't start growing.

Goal-setting

The first and most obvious question to ask yourself about your MLM business is, 'what do I want out of it?' In other words, what are your goals? The importance of thinking very long and hard over this question cannot be overemphasized. It is very easy to answer with the inevitable 'more money', but this is not specific enough. A detailed, definite goal, visualized and firmly fixed in your mind, is an essential for keeping you on the right track when your fortunes are rising and falling. Write it down, in full detail, with a date when you want it. By printing it permanently on paper you also imprint it permanently in your mind. Keep it with you and refer to it often to etch it on to your subconscious. Only five per cent of people are financially secure by the age of sixty-five, and the small number of people who write down their life's goals are among that five per cent. In business, in life, goals are essential for success. How can you be successful if you don't know what you want and when you want it?

A large corporation sets short-term goals, mid-term goals and long-term goals, and if it doesn't reach them some explanations are in order so that lessons can be learned and performance improved in the next period. Why don't people set goals for their own success in money, personal, social, spiritual, and other important matters of life? The nearest thing to this is a New Year's resolution, rarely written down and usually forgotten by the end of January. It does not matter if you do not reach your goals when you planned to. What matters is that you tried, learned from the experience, and can reset the date for attainment of those goals.

In his fascinating book, *Psycho-cybernetics*, Maxwell Maltz describes how, once you have your goal set and firmly established in your mind, it acts like the self-correcting mechanism of a modern torpedo fired at a target. Information irrelevant to the task in hand is filtered out, but every useful datum which will assist in directing the torpedo to its target is stored and used. If the torpedo begins to stray off course, its automatic correction equipment sets it back on target. The torpedo would be completely useless if it did not have an absolutely specific target programmed into its circuits, and the same goes for the human mind. Did anyone every achieve anything of worth without setting a specific target and pursuing it with a great deal of determination?

A long-term goal is essential for your success, but with this alone your short-term progress will be hard to measure. You need to make shorter-term goals too, which can be achieved, or at least strived for, within a reasonably short period, to give you encourage-ment and indicate that you are on the right track. The most successful MLM distributors have five-year, one-year, monthly and weekly goals, all written down after regular serious thinking (and discussion with their partner if they have one).

Do not confuse dreams with goals. Your dreams are what you ultimately want, your goals are the specific steps that you will have to take to achieve your dreams. For example, your long-term goals should be the level of your business that you need to reach in order to attain your dreams. Your mid-term goals should consist of the number of people in your organization that will be necessary for the sales volume that will place you at the level at which you need to be. Your shorter-term goals should be the number of people that you need to sponsor per month in order to reach the desired number for your mid-term goals, and the personal sales figures which you need to achieve and duplicate in your downline. Your shortest-term goals should be the number of people to whom you need to explain your business per week in order to reach your desired monthly sponsoring rate and sales volume.

There are good books around on goal-setting and its advantages – *see* Appendix 1 for some recommended titles.

Solid foundations

MLM is no fad or temporary convenient money-making deal which provides some extra cash for a while until something new comes along. It may be treated that way by some people, and they are at liberty to use the concept in this way, but the opportunity you have is for a serious long-term business for lifetime financial security, if that is what you want it to be. For this, though, you will have to follow some essential steps in order to build security into it. If you were constructing a building, the deeper you built the foundations, the more secure and reliable the finished construction would be. The same goes for your MLM business. There is a technique for developing strong foundations which will make your business secure, called 'working in depth'.

Imagine that you are a smooth talker capable of persuading five people a week to sign up under you in your business. In one month you have personally sponsored twenty people and you are looking forward to having a large profitable organization in a very short period. Virtually all your time is spent on sponsoring, with a bit of selling thrown in here and there, and within three months you have sponsored sixty people yourself. The strange thing that you begin to notice, however, is that your group sales volume is not developing at the rate you had hoped, and that, although your business is extremely wide, it is not getting very deep. Nobody seems to be sponsoring at anything like the rate that you are. On top of that, quite a few of your first level have quit the business already. You can't figure it out; if you can go out and sponsor sixty people in a month, surely they can do at least half of that? By the following month you are despairing – your personally-sponsored distributors are dropping out almost as fast as you can sponsor new ones.

You might be ready to quit yourself by now, but instead think about where you were going wrong. You made the assumption that most people were like you, self-motivated and dynamic, but most people are not like this at all. When you sponsor someone you give them hope that they will be able to make the business work for themselves. Most people cannot do this on their own. The whole thing is completely new to them, and they have no idea what they should be concentrating on and how exactly they should be doing it. More than anything else they need your guidance to give them information, motivation, encouragement and help. You are called a sponsor for a reason. The definition of 'sponsor' is 'a person who makes himself responsible for another'; that says it all. It is your job, indeed it is more than likely obligatory under your company's rules, to do whatever you can to assist the person you sponsored to build his business. You should do this with as many people as you can, but very few people will be able to do this satisfactorily on a part-time basis with more than about seven people. You certainly cannot do it if you are dashing around sponsoring all the time.

Your commitment does not end with your first level, if you want a truly secure organization. After sponsoring someone you will undertake to help get their business started by presenting the opportunity at the first meeting that they arrange (if you are not ready for that, *your* sponsor should be helping out). You will be teaching your new person with everything you do. They will be watching you and learning by example. You are now effecting the process of duplication, which is what makes MLM work. If you want your business to grow, you want as many people as possible to be capable of doing it. Whatever you do, your prospective distributors will look at you and ask themselves if they can do what you are doing, so you must make everything duplicable. You want nobody to look at the business and think, 'I can't do that.' The KISS method is the answer: 'Keep It Simple, Stupid.'

You have now helped your new distributor to hold his first meeting, and hopefully a further one or more have been sponsored from it. Now what? You help these new people to hold a meeting and get *their* business off the ground. You take your 'first-level' distributor with you, and when you give this presentation you are teaching him to teach others whilst teaching your second level how to hold meetings. All the time you are building strength into your organization by teaching others to teach others to teach others. No one should have to learn the long, hard, slow way by trial and error.

How many levels should you go down to in the process of working in depth? It depends on how secure you want your business to be. If your company's marketing plan pays out royalties on a certain number of levels only, I would suggest that you work quite a way below that number of levels so that you are also helping every distributor from whose volume you will be getting a royalty to build himself a secure business.

Just as you would prioritize your time each day, concentrating on the most important tasks first and doing the less important tasks afterwards, so you must ensure that your valuable time in your business is spent working with the people who are going to make the best use of it. This means working with the ones who *want* you to help them, not with the ones who don't. Of course you will not completely disregard anybody you have sponsored, but your largest portion of time must be spent on those who are going to help you build a large business in the shortest possible time.

You will not have any problem finding out who your priority people are. They will ring you with questions incessantly, and will be genuinely pleased to have you telephone them to tell them about the next meeting you have arranged at your home. They will not make excuses for not having meetings at their home. They will make absolutely sure that their house is full up with people if you have arranged to do a presentation for them. By contrast, the people you will put on the 'back burner' are those who show you that they feel you are hassling them when you offer your help. They make excuses why they cannot seriously start their business just yet. Do not waste your time trying to motivate these people into action. Your efforts are far more usefully spent in sponsoring more people of the kind you need, because the most effective motivation you can give to others is your own success. Merely let the inactive members of your group know that when they decide they want to get started seriously, you will be there to help them to the best of your ability.

Positive attitude

Possibly more important in MLM than in most other businesses is the attitude you adopt. You have read above and will read below about various qualities, the acquisition of which will assist the growth of your business. You may think that it all seems like extremely hard work to concentrate on so many things while also trying to make a go of your new business. Don't worry; you don't have to be concentrating on all these embellishments to your business from the word 'go'. Your business will grow satisfactorily if you just follow the basic principles outlined in Chapters 5 and 6. All you need from the beginning, to help you assimilate everything necessary for accelerating growth as your business develops, is a *positive attitude*.

Being positive means many things. It is a way of life rather than something you put on when you go out. It is inside you, not on the outside. Amongst a million other things, it includes:

- looking for good qualities in others;
- not criticizing, especially your spouse;
- paying compliments whenever possible;
- smiling;
- being open-minded;
- being genuinely interested in other people;
- listening more frequently than talking;
- giving;
- avoiding arguments;
- avoiding gossip.

Why does having a positive attitude assist in the growth of your business? A fundamental concept in the accumulation of wealth by any means is to secure the co-operation of other people who are able to assist you with the particular plan you have in mind to attain your financial goals. The necessary people will not seek you out themselves and offer their services to you; you will have to find them yourself and obtain their services by offering them an attractive deal. Such a deal will primarily consist of a potentially lucrative occupation and a pleasant working environment, and the latter will be gauged by them on your own appearance and attitude towards them. Negative thinking and attitudes will not achieve the result you need. They will instead repel people wherever you go. A positive personality attracts people and raises their spirits. People feel good in the presence of a positive personality. If you want to attract people to you and your MLM business, and keep them there – be positive!

A positive mind is an open mind, allowing you to learn from others and giving you the ability to look at facts and ideas without being held back by ingrained and illogical prejudices. It gives you the willingness to try new ways of living and working. These are assets to building a business of any kind, and if they are assets to your business, they will also be an asset to the business of anyone you sponsor. Positive thinking is not hereditary, it can be learned. There are many books on the subject (*see* Appendix 1), so have a look. The starting point is wanting to become a better 'you'. If there is one thing that everyone has room for, it is improvement.

MLM is all about *people*. It is about selling good products and services to satisfied customers who come back for more. It is also about sponsoring people to do the same thing. The backbone of the business is communicating with people. Communication is achieved by being the sort of person with whom people like to communicate. That sort of person is one with whom people feel comfortable, whom they feel is honest, and who makes them feel good. How do you make people feel like this? By learning and practising consistently how to become the sort of person people like. As you do this you will begin to realize that one person in particular is starting to like you more than ever before – you.

Don't get the wrong idea here; all this is not compulsory. You could build the business wearing a permanent poker face if you kept at it long enough. It is just that most of the successful people in the business will tell you that you will make it big much more quickly if you make the effort to improve the way you interact with others. You will notice benefits in every aspect of your life as you continue to improve yourself. You will make more friends, your family will be happier, you will be happier. The more likeable you are, the more people you are apt to meet and the more people will believe in you and your business.

Self-image

When you begin your MLM business you are likely to hear many disparaging comments from all sorts of people who are perhaps less knowledgeable than you are on the subject, or who are just plain negative and object to your efforts to raise your station in life. These people can very easily dishearten you if your self-image is not high enough. You must be proud of the decision you have made, because you made it on the basis of comprehensive and factual information which satisfied you of the legitimate potential of this new endeavour. You know that there are many other people around like you who will come to the same decision when you show them how your business works. You have tried the products and you believe in them, so other like people will believe in them and buy them. You *know* you have made the right decision, and your belief will keep your self-image as high as it needs to be to smile at your detractors and suggest that they ought to seek further information.

Never act, or even feel, as if you are desperate for your prospect to sign up. You may feel that a certain couple are the perfect distributors, and you've just got to have them in your team, but this is not so. You do not need any particular person or couple in order to succeed. You are going to do it with them or without them. If they want to get in and join the fun, great. If they don't, they can sit back and watch you do it anyway. If they get the feeling that you are virtually pleading with them to join, you are far less likely to get them to do so. You need to inspire them to join your winning team. Keep that self-image high and you will draw people to you. Learn to like yourself by improving yourself in all the areas of your life that need it. The more you like yourself, the more other people will like you.

Enthusiasm . . .

. . . is contagious. You cannot honestly expect a room full of people to jump up and say, 'Where's the kit?' after explaining your business wearing a miserable face. Give a presentation with obvious excitement, and you will infect the atmosphere with enthusiasm for what you have. How do you get enthusiastic? Presumably you would not have signed up in the first place if you had not been so. Enthusiasm comes from the knowledge that not only do you have a business which can provide you with the money and time you want without any great risk, but that you can also offer this business to other people who need it. The more knowledge you can obtain about the business you are in, the more you will convince yourself that it really can provide the means to realize all the dreams you have ever had. If that doesn't make you enthusiastic, turn to Chapter 2 and read again through the section on the special benefits of an MLM business.

It is a fact that most people get more excited about the prospect of saving a few pounds than making a lot of money. Take note of the story about Joe, a nice guy who declined to start an MLM business which was shown to him by his neighbour Fred. Joe is a car-oriented person, proud of his well-kept eight-year-old saloon. He goes to town one day and sees tyres for his car available at twenty pounds each when he normally pays over thirty. What a bargain! Joe has recently put new tyres on his car, but this is too good to miss. He buys four, and one for the spare, and when he gets home, having grinned all the way back from town, he bangs on Fred's door. 'Come and see what I've got. You'll never believe the price of these tyres, twenty quid each, and they're steel radials, famous brand, they'll even fit them free! You better get up there quick, before they sell out.' Fred smiles. He has shown Joe a way to make as much money as he likes, without experience, capital, or risk, yet here is his friend enthusing over the fact that he has spent a hundred pounds on something he does not even need. What riches that kind of enthusiasm could bring if directed towards something that truly deserved it!

Put things in perspective. Realize what things you have which are worth getting enthusiastic about, and you *will* be enthusiastic about them. As Ralph Waldo Emerson said, 'Nothing great was ever achieved without enthusiasm.'

Immediacy

Immediacy is the master of procrastination, the business killer. Nothing prevents businesses getting started or gaining momentum better than procrastination. The usual summary statement of the principle of immediacy is:

'DO IT NOW!'

The positive energy release experienced by following this principle can be astounding. So much time has been wasted by people thinking about and putting off decisions when they could have made the decision and got stuck into doing what the decision required of them. Countless hours have been wasted pacing up and down by the telephone worrying about how to invite people to see an MLM business. Fear is also a business killer. Fear holds people back from decisive, successful action – fear of rejection, fear of ridicule, fear of failure, even fear of success. If only you will DO IT NOW you will not allow your mind to cogitate until it finds a reason for not acting yet, or at all. DO IT NOW and the adrenalin will flow, you will think on your feet, you will not have time to be fearful, you will sound dynamic because you are being dynamic (*OED* – 'active, potent, energetic'). You will also gain great pleasure and personal satisfaction from your acts of decisiveness, not least because of their significant effect on the growth of your business. Remember:

ACTION CONQUERS FEAR.

The most financially successful people have a common trait without which they would not have got where they are. They all make decisions quickly and stick by them. The most successful people in MLM made a decision to succeed and stuck by it. When something needs doing in their business, however uncomfortable it may seem to be, they DO IT NOW without further consideration because they know it has to be done. Comfort is not an issue in building any business. Comfort is what you get when you have built it.

Change your vocabulary to fit your new decisiveness. Don't say, 'You know, we really ought to phone George and Mary about the business.' Say, 'I'm going to phone George and Mary.' Get rid of words like 'should', 'ought', 'must', 'probably', 'perhaps', 'maybe' and replace them with words like 'shall', 'will', 'definitely', 'certainly', 'yes'.

Big thinking

Nobody ever made a big success of anything by being small-minded. Thinking big means keeping the matters of most importance uppermost in your mind at all times, and not wasting your time on the unimportant. It means having big dreams to reach for and stretching yourself in order to reach them. It means avoiding pettiness and unnecessary detail and concentrating on the activities and necessary details which will help you to reach your goals. The big thinker does not waste too much time worrying about how to cut down on his or her expenditure in order to keep within a certain income level, but thinks hard about ways in which that income can be increased. There are definite limits to the amount of money which can be saved from a given income, but there are no limits to the amount of money which can be earned, given a strong desire to earn it and a method by which it can be earned.

I recently observed a classic example of the pitfalls of thinking small in business. I was a regular customer of a first-class sandwich bar in Nottingham which sold the most delicious rolls and bagels with a large selection of tasty and well-prepared fillings. The friendly and efficient owners, whose policy of keeping their customers by keeping them happy had been very successful, eventually sold out to a new owner whose principles were rather different. Cutting costs became more important than serving customers well. The selection of fillings became smaller, as did the quantity put into the sandwiches and rolls. I continued to give my custom to the place in the hope of an improvement. The turning point for me came one day when I found that there was no butter in my roll! I returned to the shop and pointed out the 'accidental' omission that had taken place, knowing that it had been a deliberate cost-cutting measure, and then I did not go there again. A few months later the place closed down. It was not just the lack of butter, but the clientele had been slowly dwindling because of similar minor irritations caused by the unproductive attitude adopted by the new owner. He had not been keeping his mind on the primary and all-important function in the building of any business, which is getting customers and keeping them.

Thinking big does not mean that you only need to think about or consider doing 'big' things. What it means is that you should also do all the little things that are essential for the realization of the big things. Because success always depends upon the co-operation of others, especially in an MLM business, it follows that time spent on helping your group with the small matters that are important to them is time well spent. The 'big' thinker is characterized by the way that he deals with 'little' people (in this context, new distributors in his business). You must be humble enough to go out and help your distributor sell his first product, if he needs you to. You must be willing to answer a late telephone call from one of your group who needs advice on any aspect of his business, and give him half an hour of your time. The way you treat your group members will be duplicated throughout your organization, to your benefit if you have treated them properly. Thinking big means not caring what people who are unimportant to your business think about your involvement in it. It does mean caring about people generally, especially those who are crucial to your business's success.

One person crucial to your success is your permanent partner, whether spouse or otherwise. It is not essential that you both build the business together, but if you are going to build it completely or mainly by yourself this should be done in harmony with your partner. This might seem obvious, but MLM businesses have failed to develop because of a negative environment created through antagonism between partners. You must bear in mind that there is no guarantee that your partner will be as excited about your new business as you are, so it is no use going headlong into it, expecting him or her to do 50 per cent of the work, and then nagging when your expectations are not fulfilled.

'If you'd sell just one product we'd start getting somewhere with this business', 'Well, if you sponsored someone it might be worth me selling something.' This type of discussion is the beginning of the end of anyone's business. Think big. Care about your partner's feelings about the venture. Before you get too involved, sit them down and discuss the whole thing. Maybe they are simply unconvinced of its potential; if so, you will have to provide it by making it work. Maybe there is a feeling that you see each other little enough as it is; perhaps you will have to give up something else in order to make time for the business. Any reasons for objecting to the business may be rational or irrational, but either way you must sort out how you are going to fit the business into your lives before you start. One thing, however, is virtually certain – when the royalty cheques start getting into four figures and doubling in value every month, few objections will remain!

Dream big and look for people with big dreams, as they are the ones who will help to give your business explosive growth. You and they will attract others with big dreams, who will be committed to reaching the very top levels in the business because they will realize that it is possible to achieve those dreams.

Being yourself

You will receive much advice when you start your MLM business, most of which will be perfectly sound, but do exercise some caution with regard to detailed instructions on selling and sponsoring. Everybody is different, and everybody feels happiest doing certain things in certain ways, including selling and sponsoring, the two prime functions of an MLM business. Sticking rigidly to a detailed specification on how to carry out these two activities is likely to have an effect opposite to that intended, because you may not be being true to yourself and to your own nature. People who know you will detect the change in your manner, be puzzled and less likely to consider the message you are trying to put across seriously. Also, if you are trying to stick to someone else's script you lose concentration and impact by being concerned with your performance.

Take to heart the basic principles of the advice and teachings you receive in the course of your business, but fit them around *you*, not the other way round. For example, improving your performance in delivering a standard script for inviting will have less impact upon your business than improving yourself and the way you interact with people generally. Be yourself, but be the best 'you' that you can possibly be. Businesswise, it is hard to teach people to act in a certain way, but it is very easy to teach them to be themselves.

When your business grows to a reasonable size you will no doubt be holding opportunity meetings for you and your group from time to time. You are going to be standing up in front of several people, telling them how the business works. This is a necessary part of the meeting, but the most effective part is when they hear your story. Nothing has more impact that personalizing the presentation, and there is no story that you can tell better than your own. When your groups hear you tell it, they will not be worried by the thought of public speaking but will look forward to telling their own story.

In every business, duplication equals success. The easier it is to duplicate your methods, the more successful your MLM business will be. So be yourself.

Professionalism

When you sign up with the MLM company of your choice, you have taken the first step in working for yourself in your own business. However small your business is, it is still a business, so you should treat it like one, because it may become a big business (if you want it to). If you act as if you have started a new hobby or a part-time activity which will give you a little extra pocket money, that is exactly the impression you will give, and that is what your business will be. It is perfectly acceptable to get into MLM for pocket money, but if you want a big business you have to treat it like a big business.

This means acting with professionalism, letting people know you are serious about the business and running it like any other successful business.

Have some smart business cards printed (your company will probably be able to supply some), and some headed notepaper. When your profits allow, install an answering machine so that you can follow up each enquiry efficiently. Always be smart when you deal with your customers. When you make a presentation in a formal situation, dress right. If you need to hire a place to give a business presentation, make it the best place you can afford, maybe a hotel suite paid for between you and members of your group. The professional approach of an impressive venue and a well-run presentation will pay for itself by convincing the prospects that what they are going to hear about is important. Naturally, not every meeting will take place in a hotel, most of them will be held in people's homes. You can still give a professional presentation in someone's lounge, and it is always worth the effort. A little extra time in preparation so that the meeting runs smoothly and efficiently is always worthwhile in terms of results obtained.

Building your business professionally also means following an established and duplicatable routine of working with the people you sponsor until you have taught them how to do the same thing properly with the people that *they* sponsor. It will not do anything for your credibility or your profitability to dish out as many kits as possible in the shortest amount of time without following up with the requisite teaching, training and motivation. Each main line of sponsorship of each good company will have a tried and tested procedure to follow, and, as far as possible within your own nature and capabilities, you should stick to that procedure for the best results and the most professional image.

Motivation and inspiration

Not only do *you* need motivation and inspiration to become successful, but so do the members of your organization. It is your job to motivate and inspire them. Motivation is not something that can be injected into a person like a vaccine, having effect for many years before a booster is needed. It is a volatile substance which must be regularly injected if it is to be effective, otherwise it evaporates, leaving you exactly where you were before you started taking it. Motivation is an internal power which drives people towards their goals. It is personal, and not only are everyone's motivating factors different, but they can change with time. In order to find out what the motivators are for the people in your own organization you must know them as well as you can. You must be able to empathize with them and find out their strengths, weaknesses, fears and desires. Only then are you able to give them what they need to motivate themselves. Make sure you can remember your people's original dreams which you may have elicited from them before you introduced them to your business. Remind them why they got into the business. Dealing with people effectively is a skill and therefore it can be learned; there are many good books on this subject, so read them, and keep reading them.

Motivation does not mean phoning your distributors every month and asking them how much they have sold. If they don't tell you to mind your own business, they will soon develop a fear of criticism from you, which is negative and destructive. What they need is nurturing and encouragement. Get together with your group regularly and help them, with what you know about them, to set goals for themselves which are just within reach. Achievement is a great motivator. If they do not reach their goals, counsel with them to find out why, and help them to reset their goals if necessary. When they are set, make sure that they know that you expect them to reach those goals. People are likely to make a greater effort if they know that someone is going to examine their results.

Incentives are good motivators, which is why most good companies always have some form of competition with an attractive prize. Some awards are staggering in their value – new cars, cruises, cash awards, gift vouchers have all been given out as prizes for outstanding effort. Only a few high achievers will manage to win this kind of gift, so why not provide your own incentives? Some very successful distributors motivate their own groups by the offer of microwave ovens, computers, even holidays. When you can afford it, such incentives will be well worth the outlay in terms of increased motivation and excitement within your group.

You have to keep yourself motivated too! Keep your dreams in mind and look at your written list of goals daily. Read motivational books and listen to motivational tapes (if you can get them!) as often as you can. Reading for five minutes every day is more effective than reading a book in two days once a month. When there is a convention or rally, make sure you get to it and that all of your group do too. There's great inspiration in a large number of people all together with similar positive aims. Successful distributors will be on stage receiving awards and telling their own stories. You will be inspired by how similar their stories are to your own, and will be reminded that success is well within your grasp.

One of the best motivators you can have (if you are reasonably strong-minded) is someone who tells you that you can't do it. You will be determined to prove them wrong. We all know somebody like this; if their ridicule and discouragement are directed at you, your ultimate satisfaction will be to do it in spite of them.

Finally, *you* can inspire your people. Be the best retailer and give them something to which they can aspire. Sponsor more people than anyone else and set an example to all of them. You want them to say to themselves, 'Good grief, if he can do it, *I* shouldn't have any problem.' The best example you can possibly give is to be successful yourself.

Association

Another principle of success is to associate with successful people. You will know from reading books on how to achieve a positive mental attitude that you should avoid people who have a negative and destructive attitude, and seek out people who can uplift and inspire you and help you to reach your goals. Successful people in MLM get where they are by applying the right principles and taking the necessary action. Don't be too awestruck by someone who earns an income twenty times greater than yours, they are normal friendly people who will go out of their way to help you follow in their footsteps (especially if you are part of their organization). Associate with them and you will appropriate some of their qualities. Ask questions of them whenever you can, find out what makes them tick and how they do the things that you find difficult in your business. You may find that they had similar challenges to those that you may be experiencing in building your business; find out how they overcame them.

Among the successful people in the business you will come across many types from different backgrounds, and with different challenges, but all with similar aspirations. You can learn, for your benefit and for the benefit of those whom you sponsor, how many different business-building challenges were overcome. When your prospects tell you why they cannot take up the opportunity, you will be able to say, 'there's a couple in our organization who had the same problem in the beginning, and now they're doing great things with their business. I'll take you to the next group meeting and introduce you to them.'

You can also learn from other people in the business many different ways of sponsoring and selling, some of which may suit you even better than the methods you are currently using. Whatever you may have been told in the beginning by your upline about how to go about selling and sponsoring, there will be many other ways to carry out these essential tasks. By associating with others you find out what works for them and you can then add their methods to your inventory for use yourself, or for recommending to those you sponsor.

Regular association with other distributors in your local group fosters a 'family' feeling, a sense of belonging to a group of like-minded people who are aiming for a common goal. They can help to lift you up when you are feeling like quitting, and can encourage you to greater heights when you are doing well. The supportive atmosphere will also keep your own distributors in the business when they might otherwise have given up. Although you should not spend too much time trying to motivate the unmotivated (far better to carry on looking for achievers), the longer they stay in the business and in contact with other distributors the better chance you will have of firing them up.

Education

Many people think that 'knowledge is power' and try to acquire as much of it as possible, wondering when they are going to achieve power, and subsequently money. Knowledge is only powerful when it is put into planned action for the achievement of a specific goal. Every businessman who wants his business to get bigger and better constantly seeks and acquires information useful or specific to him, whether deliberately or subconsciously. The same principle applies in an MLM business. The more knowledge you have about the business, the better your chance of directing it along the path you desire. Your perception of the possibilities of the business will give you the belief that you need to achieve what you want in the business. First, there is the information you can obtain from people connected with your own company, then there are other sources from which you can learn about multi-level marketing.

There are not many books on this subject (this is probably the only one written in the UK, although you can get hold of several American publications). Your company may be able to supply various reading materials, on MLM generally, and in relation to their own organization and the distributors who are part of it. There has been a recent increase in the number of good quality business opportunity periodicals, which make fascinating reading. If you have never seen one of these before you will be amazed at the quantity and variety of opportunities that exist for people to become their own boss. Often these magazines contain very helpful and informative articles which are well worth reading.

People everywhere have snippets of information which can be of use to your business. Perhaps some of your customers also buy products from distributors of other MLM companies; perhaps they are a distributor. Either way you can learn about other companies and their distributors, how they go about their business, what their products are like and how they compare with your own. There has been a tendency in the past, and to some extent it is still prevalent, for companies and their top distributors to try to shield the members of their organization and new distributors from the realities of the abundance of other opportunities available in the field of MLM. It is understandable that no company wishes to lose their distributors to another organization which may seem a more attractive proposition, but this attitude has to be unproductive.

Sooner or later in the course of building your MLM business one or more of these other schemes will be offered to you, even if only in the form of an advertisement. If you studied a substantial range of MLM opportunities before you made the decision to join your present company you will be in an excellent position to know why the scheme you are in is the best for you. If, as most people have done in the past, you joined the first scheme to which you were introduced, you need to know about this new opportunity so that you can reassure yourself that you have made the right choice. More importantly, however, you can pass this information on to your downline to reassure them that they are in the right MLM business, before they are approached by someone else. The same principle applies to other companies' products. If you get to know as much as you can about them you will be able to compare your own products fairly with others when you are selling.

The more you know about every aspect of MLM, and your own company in particular, the more confident you will become about it. You will be better able to deal with problems and challenges and better at answering questions, misunderstandings and derogatory remarks.

Delegation

Everyone has had the experience of planning a day out somewhere, intending to leave early to have as long as possible there, and then finally getting away three hours late because of all sorts of minor hold-ups, none of which were significant in themselves but which all added up to a substantial delay. This can happen in your MLM business as well if you are not guarding against it. There are all sorts of details to take care of when you are running such a set-up, some of them important, others less so. You must ensure, especially as you are likely to be building your business in addition to a full-time occupation, that most of your time is spent on the most important tasks – ie sponsoring and selling (in that order). It is so easy to get bogged down with minutiae; can someone else do it for you, while you spend the time inviting or approaching new people?

Perhaps your children, your parents, or your partner (if he or she is not fully active in the business) could be persuaded to take on some of the tasks of writing cheques, filling out order forms, keeping customer records, picking up and delivering products, keeping your accounts, typing up newsletters, making simple telephone calls, and so on? When your profits allow, you can consider employing a home help, a gardener, a decorator, a window cleaner. Whatever household tasks you do not enjoy or which take up too much valuable business-building time can be delegated as your business grows, in order to make it grow even faster.

Another type of delegation that is necessary as your business grows is the delegation of leadership responsibilities to your personally-sponsored distributors; this will help them become leaders themselves and will free your time to sponsor, train and develop others. When you first bring someone into your business you will be spending a lot of time with them, helping them to get to grips with the essentials of building a good business. This will include holding meetings for them, doing product demonstrations, presenting sales parties, and anything else they need to get off on the right track. If they are going to be ultimately successful, though, they will have to learn how to do all these things themselves so that they are able to begin training others to do them. At the right time (and you will instinctively know when this is), you will be handing over the reins to your distributors for them to carry on without you being around permanently.

Communication

When you get into MLM you will be told that you are in business *for* yourself, but not *by* yourself. When you sponsor others you will tell them the same thing. In order to keep that promise, which will benefit your business, you must be frequently in touch with all of your group. This does not necessarily mean in person every time, although there are few things better than group meetings for training and motivating. Some organizations have 'counselling' meetings once a week, some get together once a fortnight, others once a month, it's up to you. It is only worth having a meeting if there is something new to say, and you don't want your people to spend too much time at meetings rather than actively building their business. Make your meetings varied and interesting rather than lectures. Change the theme every time: sponsoring, selling, handling objections, and so on. Try to get a good speaker from time to time, perhaps successful distributors from your upline, and other motivational speakers. Get the whole meeting involved in the discussions; brainstorming an idea or a solution to a problem certainly livens up the evening.

Make sure that all the members of your group are kept up to date with what is happening within your organization, with the company, and with MLM generally. You can do this most effectively with a regular bulletin. You don't need to spend a fortune on postage sending them out to every distributor; use the MLM system to your advantage, and pass this and all other information through the structure in the same way as you do with the products. Your company is almost certain to publish a monthly distributor magazine, but your bulletin can supplement this by keeping more up to date and closer to what is happening in *your* group. Get your group members to contribute news, tips, experiences, testimonials. Success stories of close associates can be motivating, and they can be used to great effect when sponsoring.

Write short personal messages to your distributors when you can, to let them know that you have them in mind and you consider them an important part of your team. Tell them how well they are doing when you send their bonus cheque. Keep in telephone contact with your key people so that you keep track of how your business is moving from week to week.

Finally, don't forget that communication is a two-way thing. Listen to your people, know their strengths and weaknesses, how they are feeling and what their fears and concerns are. The more you know about them the more you can help them, and by helping their business you are also helping your own.

Recognition

This is a basic need of all human beings. Everyone needs to be recognized for what they achieve, however minor it may appear, and unfortunately most people do not receive recognition in their daily life for the things they do well. You do your job well, don't you? When was the last time your boss took time out to tell you? When was the last time you took home a small present for your spouse for being a great husband or wife or dad or mum? The recipient of praise does even better after receiving it. There is great satisfaction in knowing that your efforts are observed and appreciated by others.

You need to recognize your distributors' efforts because they are benefitting you. If you make them feel good for what they have done, they will do even better in future. Tell the whole of your organization when someone reaches a new level or does anything else in their business which is noteworthy. Most companies will provide various pins, plaques and other items which can be awarded to achievers in your business. When you have someone who has earned one, get them up in front of everybody else and present it to them. This may all sound a bit silly to you right now, but *it works*; it is profitable.

Integrity

You owe it to yourself, to your group and to MLM itself to run your business with the maximum of integrity. Every successful and lasting business has been built on a foundation of trust, honesty and fairness. Any fool can make short-term profits using deceit and underhandedness, but security and long-term success always require integrity. The majority of the population, including all the customers who allow you to profit by buying products from you and your organization, are fair and reasonable people. Treat them with respect, honesty and fairness, and they will come back to you again and again, they will recommend you to others and they will be the best sales promotion aid that you will ever have. The same goes for the way you treat the members of your group. Treat them right and they will make you wealthy.

Integrity is being reliable and punctual at all times, whether it involves delivering products to customers or going to do a meeting for your new distributor. It is being honest and open in answering all questions about the business and the products. It is keeping your word, paying for your products promptly and sending out bonus cheques on time. It means honouring your company's guarantees. Integrity means not using 0898 numbers in recruitment advertisements (*see* Chapter 10) and not deliberately trying to recruit other companies' distributors. It certainly means immediately rectifying any breach of your company's rules, legal requirements or any other malpractices, by a distributor in your group.

Finally, integrity involves giving people respect. If one of your group wants a small retailing business giving him £25 a week, don't try to turn him into a big businessman but respect his decision. If there is some bad news about the activities of some distributors elsewhere in the company's organization, don't keep it quiet. Give your team the respect of treating them as people who can deal with such information as well as you can. They all need to know how *not* to run their business.

Auto-suggestion

This may be a strange-sounding success principle, but it is a very important one. It is a well-researched and accepted fact that the human mind receives and stores every piece of information which comes to it at every moment of its life, and, whether or not any particular piece of it can be recalled at any time, the accumulated data is used to program the thoughts and actions of the person concerned. You have heard the saying, 'You are what you eat'; this is partly true. More accurate is, 'We become what we think about.' Your actions and attitude have been shaped by the environment in which you were brought up and in which you subsequently placed yourself, and by the information that you have fed into your mind.

This ability of the mind to affect the actions of the body can be of tremendous assistance when you decide to change your attitudes and the way you act. All you need to do is feed new 'programs' into your head on a regular basis. Whatever the mind is told often enough it will accept as truth and will act accordingly. In this chapter you have read about a number of qualities which, if acquired by you, will assist the growth of your MLM business. You can ensure the acquisition of these qualities by practising auto-suggestion.

Auto-suggestion is accomplished by the incessant drip-feeding of relevant information into the subconscious mind, in the form of statements of fact. You want to own a Porsche? Go to the Porsche dealership and sit in one, experience the feeling and the smell of it, and imagine you own it. Put a picture of it somewhere where you will see it every day. Tell yourself daily that you are a Porsche owner. Your mind will do the rest. It will direct you to take every available action which will lead to the realization of the programmed statement. If you have an MLM business, you will be directed to take the necessary steps for the accumulation of enough money to buy your Porsche.

There are established techniques for effective self-determination by means of auto-suggestion, and you should have a look at the subject. Become the person you really want to be. Whatever you want to achieve or become can be realized by self-programming, or auto-suggestion. After all, if you don't decide yourself what you want to be, you will automatically become what other people want you to be.

Summary points

1. The people who will make you wealthy *are* out there, so go out and find them!
2. Be consistent – do *something* every day.
3. Just halve the effort you put into working for someone else right now could earn you a fortune if properly directed into an MLM business. What are you waiting for?
4. Tell *everyone* about your business.
5. The best sponsoring tool is your own success.
6. Setting clear goals is important.
7. Help those who want it and find more of them; don't waste time trying to resurrect the dead.
8. Delegate, don't stagnate.
9. Give your group the respect and recognition they deserve.
10. Build a secure business by working 'deep'.
11. Are you the person *you* want to be, or are you what other people would have you be?

8: Interviews

In this chapter you will find out, from the most successful distributors themselves:

- how to sponsor new people;
- how to develop an international business;
- how to make £500 next week;
- how to make your business secure;
- how hard you have to work;
- how soon you can retire;
- what motivates them;
- success secrets of MLM.

One of the principles for success is to associate with successful people. They have done what you want to do, and can show you how it's done. You can learn from their attitude, their personality, and their straightforward and honest views on how and why they have done what they set out to do. You will have every chance to meet and talk with the most successful MLM distributors when you join a company and go to the functions that will be available, but you can learn a lot from them right now by 'listening' to them talking to me in this chapter. I have put myself in your position, which is more than likely a new or prospective distributor, and asked the sort of questions that you would probably ask of these successful people.

What are wealthy MLM distributors like? Just like you and me, and a lot of other people. They are friendly, helpful, approachable, smart, happy, positive and businesslike. You probably have all these qualities too, so why aren't you making as much money as them? What have they got that you haven't? What are the big secrets of MLM success? If you have read Chapter 7 you will have found out many of the answers. If you read the rest of this chapter you will find out some more of them.

Trevor and Jackie Lowe

Trevor (45) and Jackie (43) are Amway (UK) Ltd's top UK distributors. They are at the 'Double Diamond' level (12 or more personally-sponsored direct distributors) in the business, which they started ten years ago. They have children aged 16 and 13, and live in a large sixteenth-century house in Sussex with fourteen acres of land. They keep a few horses and drive a BMW and a Mercedes. They once tried a Rolls Royce for a while but found it impractical. It was probably used more to help out at friends' weddings than anything else! They are currently looking for a property on the Isle of Wight with a mooring for the yacht they intend to buy. The property will be used as a counselling and motivation centre for distributors in the Lowe organization. Trevor has had a pilot's licence for a number of years but has not bought his own plane because it is far easier to hire one when necessary.

Ten years ago Jackie was running a hairdressing business, but she gave it up fairly soon after their Amway business started developing fast, as it was taking up far too much valuable time. Trevor was trained as a biochemist and did four years in research with a large pharmaceutical company, which he found extremely interesting and enjoyable. Unfortunately, as many people have found, there is not much money in research. When an advertisement appeared one day for a UK representative for a West German pharmaceutical company to sell their biochemicals in this country, Trevor applied for and got the job. This was just as enjoyable as research but provided twice as much money and a company car. The company became very successful and Trevor, over the next ten years, worked his way up to becoming the general manager of a very large outfit in the UK.

Although doing very well at this point, things began to seem routine for Trevor, and when a friend of his approached him with a proposal to set up their own laboratory chemicals business, he took the plunge and went into business manufacturing and selling chemicals. The business became very successful because they had correctly identified a market need. The only trouble was that the better the business became – the more orders they received – the more difficulty they had in raising the capital to finance the production of the goods ordered. Eventually the success of the business was in fact its downfall as the cash flow problems became insurmountable. At this juncture they were approached by a large competitor company who knew the difficulties that Trevor's business was having and who made them an offer they couldn't refuse for the purchase of their company. A condition of the deal was that Trevor worked for the big company for at least two years in order to integrate the new company into the old. It was rather ironic, to say the least, for Trevor to have his company 'fail' because of its success, and have it rescued by another company which had plenty of capital, but who needed him to make the whole deal work for them.

It was around this time, 1979, that Trevor and Jackie first saw the Amway business. Trevor had been to the USA on a company trip, looking for new products to add to the company's range. He met a man from a company which dealt with a product that Trevor was very interested in obtaining for his company, and the two of them found that they got on very well. Trevor invited him to stay next time he visited England. It wasn't very long before the invitation was accepted, and during the visit he told Trevor and Jackie that he had recently started a new business which might interest them. He said that he wasn't able to explain it fully to them at that time, but that the next time they were in the USA they must visit him and he would give them all the details.

Shortly after the visit, the Lowe family took a holiday in Florida, where they looked up their friend and finally found out about the Amway business. They weren't particularly impressed. They thought that it was the sort of thing that was OK for Americans, but English people just wouldn't go for it. They were quite impressed with the concept and the products, however, and they promised their friend that they would check the whole thing out when they got back to the UK. Amway had been in the UK for six years at this time, and were not particularly big. They contacted the company and were quite impressed with the way they were treated, although they were still very sceptical about the whole thing. Nevertheless, they signed up and bought some products to try, and were also impressed with them.

'So, how did you get started?'

'My view was that we'd been in business before, I knew how to do it, I wasn't going to listen to what anyone else was saying, we were going to do this business my way. So we set about doing it like I thought the Amway business should be built and we hit the 21 per cent bonus level in three months. We then went shooting off back to the USA to tell them all over there how to do it because we were moving faster than they were. We came back and found ourselves back at the 9 per cent level, where we remained for a whole year! My view had been that if I could see the business once, buy a kit and then go out and sell products, then everybody else could do it too. When I showed the business to people it was, 'I want to show you the Amway business, this is how it works – blah blah blah – do you want to get in?' If they said yes I sold them a kit and then left them with it. If they said no I said, 'Do you want to buy some products?' That was it, I didn't do anything else. The result, of course, was that, for the majority of the people that we introduced, they bought some products the first month, their volume shot up and therefore so did ours, but they had no means of continuing to build the business so it just all faded away. They didn't service their customers properly and they didn't sponsor people because they had no support and they didn't know what to do.

'After a year of getting fed up with it and thinking that it didn't really work after all, we went back to the USA to see our sponsors and said, 'OK guys, what is it we're doing wrong?' They said, 'We thought you'd never ask.' They explained to us in detail what they were doing in the USA and suddenly it all fell into place. What we had not been doing was providing distributors with a system which, when they made a decision to start their Amway business, they could get on board and use to help them to build. The critical element of that system was what we call 'driving a leg in depth', where, when you show the plan to somebody and they decide that they want to start their Amway business, one of the first things you do for them is arrange some meetings for them, and show the plan for them, because they're brand new and don't know how to do it. If they invite a house full of people and you show the plan to them, you identify at least one of the people there who wants to get in, and you go and do the same for them. You show the plan for them and get them building. So you keep on going down and down because if you are the leader of a growing group, constantly working down through your group, you are helping *all* the people in your group.

You are setting a very good example for everybody because if they will only do the same as you're doing then you get good growth. You're maintaining the 'duplicatability' of the business because you're there showing the people what they should be doing, you're meeting the people in the group so you know them, which helps to develop group unity which is good for communication, which holds people into the business and provides them with an accurate track to run on. It tends to prevent people running off and doing crazy things. That concept which we learnt made all the difference. As soon as we came back and started to put that in place the business was just great.'

'So how far down the group do you go?'
'You keep going down until you have a direct distributor with a direct distributor in depth. Generally speaking, a "leg" is secure at this point. Of course, you are also building a number of other legs at the same time.'

'But how many can you do that with at once?'
'Well, I think a comfortable maximum is seven active legs. Also, if you have seven active legs you will find that you are keeping a good percentage of your bonus cheque. We found that with seven active legs you will be keeping at least 50 per cent of your bonus cheque. The target is between 55 per cent and 60 per cent, but it depends on exactly how the legs develop as to how the money actually works out.'

'When you started doing the business the "wrong" way were you having meetings?'
'Oh yes, but the point was that we'd show people the plan and on the night we'd say to them, "Do you want to get in?" We don't say that now, we say, "Look, you can't get in tonight. We're going to show you this idea, if you like it we've got some literature for you to take away. Study it, and we'll get back to you in a couple of days' time. If you don't like the idea, no hard feelings." We don't put people under pressure to do anything. In the beginning we did, and if they weren't interested that was it, nothing more was done. If they did get in, still nothing was done, we just gave them a kit. That's why we had such rapid growth, because we sponsored a lot of people, and

it all went downhill because we hadn't shown them what to do. The whole point about multi-level marketing, and the Amway business in particular, is that you can build a large, secure and permanent business; but it can only be secure and permanent if you build an organization of sufficient size to iron out all the wrinkles, the ups and downs, the different volumes from one month to the next.'

'How big does your business have to be before you can say it is secure?'
'My theory is that when you have built your business to the Ruby level, that's around £11000 of retail sales per month, and you have a direct distributor in your group, you could then disappear and your business would still grow. There is definitely a point where the business is self-sustaining, and it is somewhere around the Ruby level.'

'When you started your business you were having meeting after meeting after meeting; did you get to the point where you didn't have any more people left on your list to invite to any more meetings?'
'No, not at all. That's not the point, you see, what we were primarily looking for was seven active legs, so all of our work was working in depth and we didn't need at that time to put in any more personally, so the ones on our prospect list were still sitting to one side. Today we still have people we could have shown the plan to ten years ago and we haven't shown it to them yet! It's not the business of putting a mass of people in personally. If you sponsor fifteen to twenty personally, you will typically find three people out of those who will pick up the business and run with it straight away. Within a two- to five-year period of time, out of the fifteen or twenty you will find another three who didn't do a lot to start with but who hung on and something sparked them off some time later. So a business fifteen to twenty wide, over a two- to five-year period, will give you six direct legs. The better way of doing it, however, is to put in the fifteen to twenty wide, find out who your three active ones are, and then put in some more so that you in fact have six or seven active ones. You'll be really busy but you'll get through to the Diamond level more quickly.'

'What size of meetings did you have?'

'As large as possible. We've shown a lot of plans. The smallest meetings we've had is when there's been no one there except ourselves, and the biggest one was an occasion when we said to some new people that we would go and do their first meeting for them the next week, telling them to invite as many people as they could. When we arrived at this address we thought that there must have been a party going on because there was nowhere to park. It turned out that the 'party' was at the house we were going to. So many people had turned up that they couldn't get all the people into the house! We spent an hour getting people sorted out with different meeting dates! I suppose the average size of meeting – averages are always misleading of course because it's being average that keeps the average down – was about two or three couples.'

'You still have meetings?'

'Yes we do because we're still working in depth in some areas which we are still trying to develop.'

'When you are inviting or approaching people do you still use the same sort of methods that you used ten years ago?'

'No. One of the things our USA upline was doing ten years ago was using what was known as the "curiosity" approach, which basically was that you didn't admit that it was the Amway business. This was based upon the concept that in the USA everybody knew about Amway and everybody had a bad impression of it, which was pretty negative thinking. However, that's what we did, and if somebody said, "Is this Amway?", you'd say, "Airway? No, it's not Airway." Terrible, pretty terrible. We realized after a while that it was a stupid thing to do because there was no bad connotation with the Amway business in the UK, very few people knew about it, and if we persisted in using that approach we would create our own "negative". So we made the very conscious decision to differentiate what we did from what our USA upline did, and openly invited people to see the Amway business.

'So if I was inviting you along I would first of all find out if you were looking for something. There's no point in showing the business to somebody who's not looking for something. I would want to try to identify something, such as what you wanted to get out of your job, or that you wanted to be able to take care of an increased mortgage, or that you wanted to take a special holiday, buy a new car, something like that. I would say to you, "It's very interesting what you're saying Peter. I can't promise you anything but I think I might be able to help you because I'm working with a couple of people right now who have similar objectives to yourself. I'm showing them how I've developed my own Amway business, which is a network marketing business, and you could do exactly the same and that would give you, if you work at it, the additional income you require." That's how I invite people, and what they usually say is, "Amway? What's that?" If they say, "Amway? Oh, I've heard about that," I say, "Fine, if you know something about it then we need to get together." Very occasionally they say, "Oh, Amway, I've heard all about that, I'm just not interested," and I'll say, "Hey, hold on a second, I don't know what you've heard or what you've seen in the past, but I know that what I'm doing in my own Amway business you can do in your Amway business, and it could give you what you just said you were looking for. Isn't it worth an hour and a half of your time to take a look?" That's a pretty powerful invitation.'

'Everybody must be nervous of approaching people when they first get in the business?'
'Sure, I've got over that now, obviously. Our biggest challenge now in our business is that every week we've got people actually phoning us up and saying, "Look, when are you going to show us that business you told us about?" I actually have to hold myself back when I meet people now! This does illustrate the point that if you'll just do the work in the beginning . . . a feature of the Amway business is that the toughest work is in the beginning and it gets progressively easier and easier as you go along.'

'What would you say to someone who is just too scared to pick up their telephone and invite someone?'
'We have a little system which will take care of that, we call it a "quality invitation". Let's suppose I had arranged to come and do a first meeting for you, and I turn up at your place and you're sitting there saying, "I don't think there's anybody coming tonight." I will say, "Well let's make some good use of the evening anyway." In

conversation I discover that the problem is that you felt very uncomfortable about getting on the telephone. I would ask you if you had written a prospect list. If you hadn't we would talk about how you could draw one up, and then when you had some names on the list I would say, "Look, why don't you just call this guy here at the top of this list, and all I want you to do is introduce me to him on the phone, saying you've got a friend here who's very excited about a business venture which you're getting keyed up about too. Say we were just discussing him and that we think he'd be absolutely perfect for it, then hand him over to me, giving him my name. I'll say, "Hi, George. Pete tells me that you would be very excited about the possibility of developing some extra income," and I would just talk to him and invite him. The ideal scenario is when I say to George, "You're not too far away from here are you? What are you doing right now? Can we get together?" With any luck we can get in the car, go to George's and show him the plan.'

'A lot of people think that if they get into the business they are going to be hassled to sell, sell, sell.'

'I have to say that in some groups that does happen because anyone can start an Amway business and start sponsoring people and hassle them. We try to teach that most definitely that's the last thing you do. You create the environment which holds them in there. You create that environment by making it comfortable for them to participate if they choose to, and by providing them with information and a system that they can pick up and use at any time.

'If you sponsored somebody who did nothing for a year, how would you keep in contact with them?'

'We have a regular list printed of our meeting dates which we would send them every three months, we would send a letter with that saying it would be good to see them and if they need any help to give us a call. We would probably call them maybe every couple of months to see if they needed anything, just simply to maintain contact. At renewal time we would send them a letter pointing out that if they don't think they'll be doing anything in the next year, that's fine, but it would be a good idea for them to renew so that if their circumstances change they can pick up and run with the business straight away because they are still distributors, and also that they can continue to buy the products at wholesale.'

'In this year's letter to your group you say, among other things, that if someone wants to make £500 next week you can show them how. How can they do that?'
'Well, one of the special features of the Amway business is that it's a very flexible idea and you can adapt it and use it to achieve whatever you want to achieve. For example, a lot of people would be looking at the business because they need to make money straight away. The only way they can make money straight away is to develop some retail volume straight away. So in this instance we would sit down with you and train you how to go out and do party-plan selling of perfumes or decor every night of the week, and I'm quite sure that you would have generated £500 by the end of that week. A lot of people don't choose to do that, it's not a good way of building the business for the long term, because if you do that this week, you might be able to do it next week, but can you do it every week? It can be done, but there are better ways of building that sort of weekly income with some security too, and that's by building an organization. So those people who start off having a need for a lot of cash, you have to talk to them only about retail selling because that's the only way to generate large amounts of immediate income.

'My view on the business when I looked at it was that I didn't care if I made any money for two years because when I saw the sales and marketing plan I didn't look at it from the point of view of generating immediate income. What I needed was something in the medium and long term which was permanent, which was my own business, and which would make good money in the long term. That's a good illustration of the flexibility of the business.'

'How hard do you have to work to make it to the Diamond level? How many hours a week?'
'We had this year-long period when there was not a lot happening at first, until we went back to the USA and got ourselves organized properly. As soon as we started to apply this principle of developing in depth, things started to grow rapidly, and as I saw it grow I realized that I could ensure that the job I was in was my last job. So I got serious about it, and we were then out working this business

five and six nights a week. We did that for a bit over a year and then I was able to leave my job, because I didn't need it anymore, and we were full time in the Amway business.'

'How did you and Jackie split the work between you?'
'Well, I would show the plan, she would do a product demonstration, she would deal with questions about retailing and things like that and I would deal with questions on inviting and stuff like that.'

'Did you have children at this time?'
'Yes, two young kids.'

'How did you deal with getting them looked after in the evenings when you were building the business?'
'The big benefit with young children was that they were in bed before we went out to a meeting, so it didn't really matter too much if we weren't there if we had a babysitter whom we had confidence in. It really wasn't a challenge. We were quite happy doing what we were doing in the short term because it meant that in the long term we would have much more time with the kids. In my last job I had to get up at seven in the morning and I got back at seven in the evening, so when they were young I probably didn't even see them until the weekend. So becoming independent and free from a nine to five job meant that I could see the kids during the day. It was short-term inconvenience for long-term convenience.'

'Was it all hard work?'
'No. I think that at the time it probably seemed occasionally like hard work but after the event it was easy to look back and realize that it was a piece of cake. When you consider that the Diamond level gives you a very good income, you can be financially free and independent and virtually retired because the amount of work you have to do in an Amway business is not like a nine to five job at all in terms of hours per week; far from it. When you look back and see what you had to do to get to that point it's not a whole lot of work. You didn't have to do a seven-year university course or get 'A' levels or anything.'

*'So five or six nights a week for a bit over a year to make
Diamond? Seems like a reasonable deal.'*
'Yes, a reasonable deal.'

*'Suppose somebody can only spare one night a week,
just a few hours?'*
'They can still do the business. If they were really serious and
committed it would probably take them five years to go Diamond.
That's not a bad deal either. They are going to have some challenges
that you don't have when you're pumping it hard. The challenge
they face is the one of time slipping by and the old syndrome of two
steps forward and one step back. Momentum is a key word in the
Amway business. The more you've got happening around you the
better, because it means that other people who are involved with
you see what's going on and they become more active. If you've only
got a low level of activity then it doesn't have the urgency, and the
people you've introduced into the group don't have that urgency.
That's why we say sponsor fifteen or twenty at your level of
commitment or above. This business does not work by going and
putting up a board in the dole queues and saying, "Hey, I want to
show you something." People in dole queues need a job, they don't
need the Amway business. When they've got a job, then they need
the business.'

'What sort of income can a Diamond expect?'
'It depends on the structure of their business. It is theoretically
possible to have a Diamond pin and make £21000 a year, but that's
the worst it could possibly be. To answer your question I would
anticipate that it would be a pretty lousy business if you didn't earn
£30000 in your first year as a Diamond. If you do it sensibly and
build it big and deep, you ought to be able to do £40000 to £45000
in your first year as a Diamond.'

*'How quickly could someone build a business to the point
where he could leave it to carry on by itself, without
putting any more work into it?'*
'You need two permanently qualified direct distributors, that makes
you a permanently qualified direct. So if you retired then, you would
still receive the 3 per cent bonus; that's permanent income.'

'How good at selling do you have to be?'
'You don't have to be good at selling at all. The principle we use on selling products is that we demonstrate them and ask people if they would like to try them; that is not selling. When you've got a 100 per cent money-back guarantee it's just as if every first purchase is a sample.'

'How much effort do you put into selling these days?'
'We've been in the business so long that our base of customers are well trained and most of our customers will call us regularly for products. I had one call me today. In the beginning you have to put some effort into it, you've got to give them the service, but eventually your customers will become hooked on what we have, which are good products.'

'What's the best way to get customers?'
'If you're looking at developing a big business the best way to get new customers is to show the plan, and those people who don't want to get in, asking them if they would like to use the products. If your needs are different, and you need to make a lot of money straight away then you have to do some different things. You have to organize some product presentations, party-plan selling or whatever.'

'There are so many products and services in the Amway business now, how does a new person decide which ones to concentrate on?'
'That's a very good question. I don't fully know the answer to that. What we practise is to tell people that the core of our business has always been the home care products, the sort of things that you will be using tomorrow. If you start with those and get experience of using them, you'll think they're good and you'll want to sell them. As time goes on you will find out which other areas you are interested in and we can then arrange for you to get some training in selling these other products.'

'What would you say was the most important quality for anyone to have in order to build a successful business?'
'Stickability. Consistency. It's so simple, all you've got to do is show

the idea to people, sponsor the ones who want to do it, sell products to the ones who don't. That is so simple that everybody can do it. I know that for a fact, anyone can do it. The thing that makes the difference is if they stick at it long enough to make it worthwhile.'

'How much do you personally sell each month?'
'We do between £150 and £200 worth of products per month.'

'What sort of training do you give your group?'
'We like to create the environment that holds people in the business long enough for them to make it. It helps them to be consistent. We have fairly regular get-togethers of one type or another. The basic one is a counselling meeting twice a month. Each direct distributor will do one of those, they will talk to distributors about attitudes, products, how to introduce people, how to show the plan, lots of things, for about an hour. Then it will be just a general get-together, coffee, biscuits, and so on. We then do some more advanced meetings; we have a 9 per cent leadership meeting where the directors talk to the emerging leaders in their group.

'Every three months we have a seminar and rally for all distributors to attend, when we'll bring in a "big pin" from somewhere, maybe the USA or New Zealand or maybe the UK. They will talk about the things they found important in building their business, and their background, their story. It gives people a different view, a different slice of the business. A lot of this material is recorded and put out on tapes on a regular basis, we regard this as being a constant connection with the business. If people are getting some input about the business on a regular basis they are more likely to stay interested in it, more plugged in. We also supply a whole series of excellent motivational books. Finally, twice a year we do weekend functions, a "dream weekend" in January and a "family reunion" in July. That's where we all get together at a central location like a hotel, and have a function interspersed with some business, some entertainment, some guest speakers. Because it's a weekend function and people are with each other, eating together, it develops good strong relationships, which tend to help people to stay in the business.'

'If a person is going to all the meetings, all the rallies,
buying all the recommended tapes and books – it's going
to cost them a lot of money, possibly more than they are
making in the business.'

'Suppose you were in a situation where you had to make £500 next week. It would not be appropriate for you to use any of the facilities, which are all long-term facilities. So if you were a brand-new person we wouldn't even talk to you about those. However, if you were not bothered about instant profitability, but wanted to build a big business, the first thing I would say to you would be to get into the tapes, the books, the functions.'

'Why pick Amway, when there's a lot of multi-level
marketing companies to choose from?'

'It's been around a while. It's been well tried and tested. It has the best plan I've seen because it pays bonuses on all generations in depth for all time. It has an extensive product range and it is international.'

'What keeps you going now?'

'After the money aspect, when you're working with people, helping them to achieve what they want to achieve, it is absolutely fantastic. I've known Alec and Brenda Wills [newly-qualified Diamonds] for years and Alec was a headmaster who was forced to retire early because he had had three heart attacks. When I met Alec after he had come out of hospital, realizing that he would never work again, he was not a happy man. But now, about eight years later, when he's been working hard and enjoying every minute of it . . . that is really terrific when you see that sort of thing happen. We're seeing that sort of thing all the time, we see people getting excited as their business grows, it's very motivational.'

'How many plans do you have to show to make Diamond?'

'If you show the plan a hundred times you'll be at the 21 per cent level. That doesn't always work out, but it's not far off. So I reckon that if you show the plan between 600 and 1000 times you will be very comfortably Diamond.'

> *'What's the width of your business?'*
>
> 'We're paying out 38 bonus cheques every month, plus there's 16 directs who deal with the company.'

> *'When will you be Triple Diamonds?'*
>
> 'Soon!'

Gigi Field and Neil Verlander

Neil and Gigi are at the time of writing the number one distributors for L'Arome (UK) Ltd, a company specializing in perfumes. They live in a small village in the heart of Worcestershire in a comfortable and unpretentious detached house. From outside the only things that give them away as being extremely successful multi-level marketers are the two new and expensive cars sitting out front, each bearing a L'Arome sticker on the rear. In the first twenty minutes of meeting Neil and Gigi I managed to get in about two minutes of conversation between the incessant telephone calls and fax messages from excited distributors in their group.

Neil was trained as a mechanic and did a succession of jobs with small firms until he decided that he was getting a bad deal. He had not been able to get his City and Guilds qualification as none of his employers had been able to afford to send him to college. After three years of apprenticeship he was only earning £12 a week, yet friends of his in other areas of work were earning £12 a day. He got married and became a father, and then joined the Army, taking his family with him. Unfortunately this did not work out and the result was a divorce. After seven years in the Army, and a year after meeting Gigi, he bought himself out and went to live with Gigi and her parents. Then followed a variety of jobs, firstly as a motorcycle courier, then as a salesman for coffee machines (he managed to sell one of them in his first six weeks!).

The next job was with a DIY sales company, through an advertisement in the local job centre. Although enjoyable, the pay was not too good and Neil soon found himself working for a company which sold home security equipment. He did well with this firm but eventually decided to go into partnership with one of his customers in a venture involving low-energy decorative lighting for public houses and commercial premises, something that is popular now, but wasn't at that time. A year was spent on this, with no income until it was time to call it a day. In another partnership they bought a squash club in Worcester. They moved there and began the hardest two years of their lives. Within three weeks of starting the venture they knew they were going to lose money on the whole thing. They managed to build it up somewhat and finally sold it, leaving themselves in debt to the tune of £25000. They were at a low point.

They had been involved with an MLM company about ten years previously, had enjoyed the social aspects of it, and could see the potential of the concept but for various reasons hadn't been able to develop it significantly. In order to help claw his way back up, Neil turned again to MLM and joined another company after answering an advertisement in a paper. Their sponsors encouraged them to find £2500, which came from Gigi's savings, to buy stock in order to obtain maximum discount; a practice which the Government's new regulations aim to discourage. After the initial enthusiasm it became hard for them to encourage others to invest so much money in stock, having been in great debt themselves before. They became uncomfortable with the way the business was being developed in the UK and finally left it.

Gigi was an account manager for a communications company for seven years before seeing the L'Arome business. She was virtually supporting Neil, a divorcee with two teenage sons, when he came out of the Army and was looking for a business of his own.

'How were you sponsored into L'Arome?'

Neil: 'A guy that I had become acquainted with through someone I knew during my time with the other MLM company telephoned me one day and asked me if I had seen L'Arome. I said I'd never heard of it and he said that it was a new British multi-level company. I said I wasn't interested. I spoke to him the following day and again he mentioned L'Arome. He did this for nearly two weeks and ignored all my efforts to get him to go away and leave me alone. Finally I said I would send him £25 for a kit on condition that he didn't phone me anymore. That was it, the kit came through, I looked at it, I was intrigued by it. Gigi wasn't at all impressed. She didn't sign up and made me promise that I wouldn't do it. The kit stayed in the house for three days, a guy came round for a cup of coffee, looked at the kit and said, "My wife would love to do that." Then I was down at the squash club with a neighbour, taking the mickey out of my body-builder friend for starting a perfume business, when he said, "Why don't you bring the kit round because my wife likes perfume?" Blow me down if she doesn't want a kit too. So I've got a body-builder and a floor-layer as my first two distributors.

'It impressed me because they had no special talents, no experience, neither of them were salespeople, and they got to the top level. In two months we had qualified as group directors. We went away to Cyprus at the end of our second month, and when we came back we were group directors.'

'When did you decide to make a commitment to the business?'

Gigi: 'November 1987. Before then I wasn't at all interested, I wouldn't wear the perfume, I hated it if there were any distributors in the house when I got home, because I felt that multi-level marketing wasn't going to deliver, and get us out of the problems we were in. We owed money to the bank, I hated the cottage we were living in and thought we would never get out of it. When we got back from Cyprus and we were at 45 per cent, we talked about it and said, "Look, we really ought to roll with this because of Christmas coming up.' We started sponsoring people we knew, using the basic rule of making a list and contacting everyone on it. We went through old diaries, I went through my mum's diary! I would just tell them what we were doing and ask if I could send them some literature. Not everybody joined. I was at work, I sponsored a couple of people from work and it just began to grow from there. So we worked at it, did some sponsoring, got some parties cooking and did about £17000 worth of business that month.'

'Did you do any advertising for distributors?'

Neil: 'We didn't do any advertising until about five months after we started. Advertising works but it is difficult and expensive as a way of building a group.'

'What is the level of your personal sales?'
Neil: 'Personal retail sales have never been major. The whole thing is about a lot of people each moving a little. We have had maybe eight or ten customers a month over the whole 27 months, but that's enough. We have people who do a lot of selling, there's a party-plan outlet for this product. We have ladies in our team who go out and do two, three, four parties a week and make immense profit.'

'Would you attempt to recruit at a party?'
'Oh always, everywhere, anywhere, every opportunity that we have.'

'So the answer to the question, "How do you sponsor?" is ...'

'Anyway you can!'

'Do you have "opportunity" meetings?'
'Yes, we started off in our house, a few people round to "have a look at this". Then we did other people's houses – "you get some people round and we'll come and show them the business."'

'You tell people exactly what it is they're coming round to see?'
'There's nothing more embarrassing than to have somebody come round and say, "I've seen this and I'm not interested. Why didn't you tell me what it was?" I can do without that. I want people to know what it is I've got, why I'm doing it and what's in it for them before they come.'

'What did you say to people that you called up?'
Gigi: 'We've found that the best way is to be honest. We'll say something like, "Listen, we've come across this company L'Arome, it's worth looking at. It may not be for you, but this is what we're doing, I seem to like it, I like the products ..." Just tell the story as it is, use the video, use the other tools. We never use scripts when we talk to people on the telephone, it's false. I remember doing it when we were in another MLM. I rang someone with my upline

standing there looking over me, I was absolutely fear-struck. I read the script to this friend of mine; she thought I'd gone demented.'

Neil: 'It's easy to teach people to be themselves. The majority of people couldn't do a telephone script, and if they got a question at the other end they would fall off the script anyway.'

[At this point a fax message came through from two of their distributors.]

Neil: 'L'Arome has just had a 90-day incentive programme, the top three personal group volumes accumulated over three months are awarded a Fiesta, an Escort and an XR3i. Two of our guys won two out of the three cars. This young couple were £70 a week hairdressers, look what they've got now. They're a lovely couple, so much success for such a young age [23].'

Neil brought out their 'How to' folder, which they take with them wherever they go, in addition to wearing their 'Ask me How to' badges. This guarantees enquiries from people they meet. 'How to what?' is answered by, 'How to make more money or save more money. Which do you prefer?'

The folder contains pictures and diagrams which can be used to give a five-minute presentation of the business, and pictures of the homes and cars they owned before and after joining L'Arome. Copies of their royalty cheques for each month show a fairly steady increase from around £1000 in their second month to their best-ever month recently, which just topped £30000. That's without the royalties from Australia, New Zealand and Ireland.

Neil: 'The danger people have when they are communicating in conversations is that they don't use the power of the picture. It gives someone who isn't used to presenting, which is probably the majority of people, a format to help them show the full extent of the business, quickly.'

Gigi: 'If I'm trying to promote to you a part-time business and it takes me three hours to do it, that's not part-time. L'Arome give you a thirty-minute video which I can give to someone and say, "Do me a favour, have a look at this video, it may not be for you, I need it back tomorrow." If they are interested after they've seen it I'll give them a copy of the Business Booster and invite them to a meeting. We're up-front, there's no secrecy.'

'Do you set yourselves goals?'

Gigi: 'Even when we were down and out we would still go and look at £100000 houses, go to the garages and sit in Porsches and Mercedes. A picture of the bathroom we now have was on the wall at one time, the kitchen was on the wall at one time, the Mercedes has been on the wall. They've all been on the wall, we've set goals for a long, long time. It's a major asset that a lot of people miss in MLM.'

[On the upstairs office noticeboard at present is a picture of a Honda Goldwing motorcycle.]

'What about training for your group?'

Neil: 'Well, we don't over-train. We do little meetings in certain areas, like in Worcester we'll do one a fortnight in a nice little room in a pub. There'll be maybe a thirty-minute first bit which is for new people. We will help them if they have trouble explaining their business to people. It is also for people who, if they don't have the facilities at home to be able to invite people round, can bring them there. It brings everyone together regularly to expose them to other people's successes. In the second half, after people have got themselves a drink, we have some simple training; how to carry the kit around and what to say when people ask about it, the sort of problems they're going to get on a day-to-day basis.'

'What does your organization look like?'

[Neil held up a computer printout which listed all of their first, second, third and fourth level group directors. It was about eight feet long.]

'There are seventeen personally sponsored. Some others have been lost along the way. These are the active ones.'

'How do you go about starting an international business?'

'You build in the UK. When L'Arome launched in Ireland we didn't know a soul there but we got an income from there because somebody in our group knew someone in Ireland, and they were within our four group director levels. I went to Australia because I've got three brothers there. I went to sponsor all three; one wouldn't do it, one signed up because I hadn't seen him for thirty years and the other one, who I didn't think would sign up because he was the wealthiest, signed up and made group director. We sponsored four people there and our first royalty cheque was A\$6000. When you expand internationally you can do it yourself; say you and I sponsored in America, we'd get a result. If we went round a group of a thousand people and said, "Who do you know in America? Here's some information, this is what you want to do, talk to everybody, write to them, phone them, do what you want to do," we could interest, out of that thousand people, maybe two hundred Americans. So we've got ourselves a business. Everybody's only sent about eighty pence worth of information instead of one person sending eight hundred quid's worth.'

'Do you get royalties on international business started by one of your fourth-level group directors?'
Neil: 'I'll get royalties on their wholesale volume, yes, up until somebody breaks at the fifth level. People shouldn't just work down within their "pay line" [the last level that generates royalties], you really want your four levels to have four levels of their own. I want all my four levels to have as big a business as possible, because that gives me security. So we actually work down below our pay levels.'

'What keeps you going? You're doing pretty well, so what's the incentive for you in 1990?'
Neil: 'We want to be the first ones we know of to have a £50000 a month royalty cheque. Our target in 1989 was to get to £30000 and we just made it. We'd like to have a million pounds income in 1991. Really there's so many things; there's that motorbike up there, there'll be a change of house, which we're planning. I've always wanted a house with a snooker table in it, an indoor swimming pool, and I'd like about ten or twelve acres of land, I'd love to have a wood. We can't realize it yet, it's too early because we're still in awe of what we've achieved. In two years, although there have been material changes, the believability for us is still difficult. We're here in this fabulous house with a small mortgage, everything's paid for, we paid for the bathroom cash, we paid for the kitchen cash, there's a

triple garage being built, and it's like we're sat here still soaking it in because it's incredible growth. We've earned £355000 in our first two years.'

'How hard have you worked?'

Neil: 'There's a difference between working hard and working smart. It's easy for anybody to work hard, but it's a blend of both. You have to work hard but smart. You're not clever by working hard, the key is to get people to duplicate what you do. We work hard, believe me, but we make sure we enjoy our work and when we feel we're tired and we're under stress we take time out.

'What do you think is the reason for L'Arome and some of their distributors having been so successful so quickly?'

Neil: 'The management is proven. For any four people to take something from nothing to forty million pounds turnover in four countries, and develop the internal management, the resources, co-ordinate something like eighty-odd suppliers, that's good management. L'Arome definitely have the management, the product and the marketing plan right. With these products you've got a minimum price of £4.99, a maximum price of £11.99, versus a comparative product at double or triple that price, so already we're below normal price, and that's in our favour. It doesn't take a skill to sell perfume, we don't sell it, people buy it.'

[Forty-eight days after our interview, Neil and Gigi put a deposit on the Honda Goldwing!]

Trevor Mitchell

Trevor is single and 35 years old. He has been a Kleeneze agent for fifteen years and is an executive distributor with the company. He lives in Bangor, County Down, in a house with its own office and garage, and drives a Mercedes car which he changes every two years. Shortly he will replace his present car with a 250 or a 300 model. He goes on holiday whenever he wants to, and has been to Canada, Mexico, Hawaii, and Alaska. His income from his Kleeneze business allows him to buy virtually anything he wants without having to think too much about it. His hobbies are computing (he has a BSc honours degree in this line) and stamp-collecting.

'How did you come to work with Kleeneze?'

'I was nineteen and at university. We had bought Kleeneze products at home in Bangor for years and years and years, and we thought we knew about the company. The agent had been one of the original suitcase salesmen, but at that time he was bringing one or two products and demonstrating them. We never realized that there was a lot more in the range than what we were buying, or that Kleeneze was a multi-level marketing company. He was with the company for nineteen years and retired at 65, but our next-door neighbour wanted to buy the washing powder and couldn't get it anymore, so she wrote to the company.

'Shortly after, one of the company executives from Scotland came to supply some washing powder to her and asked her if she would like to become an agent. She said she didn't have the time, but when he asked her if she knew of anyone else who would be interested she said to go and see the chap next door. I wasn't in when he called but he was quite persuasive with my parents and left one of the starter packs. I got home that night and I was signed up as a Kleeneze agent. Now I thought I knew Kleeneze then but when I read the manual I realized that you could sponsor other agents. I wasn't remotely interested in selling, but in my first week I went out and sponsored that next-door neighbour who had said no! I then set up a cousin and an aunt, and in my second week I had an advert in our local paper for agents.'

'How did you approach them?'

'I went to them individually and told them about Kleeneze and how they could build up a business, and the girl who had recommended me was interested in how I was getting on and wanted to know all about it. The more I told her, the more interested she became. She became an agent and did quite well. I realized from day one that money was to be made at sponsoring, not door-knocking, and I didn't have the slightest interest in that; I wanted to build the business up. At that time I was on a sandwich course, a year out in industry. I was doing computer science at Belfast and working in the Civil Service as a computer programmer when this all happened. I built the business up gradually and then went back for the final year to graduate, and when I graduated I just went straight into the business full-time. Another point which is interesting is that if I had not had sponsored agents, if I had just gone door-knocking, I wouldn't have made any income from the business in that final year when I went back to university. But because all the energy was put into getting agents I was still making money from the business.'

'*So you've never been in anything else?*'
'No. I don't want to be because I've absolutely no regrets, no regrets financially, I've travelled the world. I'm just back from the USA; the funny thing about it was that the group had the best month ever when I was away!'

'*So how have you sponsored most of your distributors?*'
'Most of it is actually through advertisements. The first twenty people I interviewed, every one of them signed up! I keep a small classified advertisement going, something like, "Turn spare time into spare cash, write or phone for details." The trouble with the telephone is that if you're not in they don't phone back, and if you are in they want to know all the details and then they say they'll get back to you and never do. So I had an extra telephone line put in with a permanent answering machine which asks for the caller's full name and postal address, which they willingly give. Then I just go and knock on their door unannounced. Most of them let me in, if it's inconvenient I will try to arrange a convenient time for an interview.'

'*Is there not a danger of too many Kleeneze advertisements appearing, if your downline advertise as well?*'
'Not really. In the welcome tape that everybody gets when they start we solicit them to make a list of names of people that they know and would like to share the opportunity with. We always start people off with prospects whom they know, the advertising can come later. When several agents in one town wish to advertise we combine it into one large advertisement. We've got a young lad in Belfast, he's seventeen, within a month he'd started ten people as agents, and those ten people are all school pals, not one of them was from an

advertisement. There's another young lad, the year after he left school he was actually in Torremolinos at conference! And we have some good examples of family businesses, there's a chap who's done fifty years in the business and his father was in the business, his brother is and his grandson is.'

> *'You have sponsored three 22 per cent groups. How many others have you personally sponsored?'*

'Well, there's five main agents and another chap who's been with me for fourteen years, the others come and go as they please depending on when they need some money. We get a lot of people who want the products but who have lost touch with their agent. They telephone the company and they are told that they will get their goods delivered although there is no Kleeneze agent within twenty miles of them. Then they are asked if they know anyone who would be interested in becoming an agent for the area. In many cases they then become an agent themselves. The people we seem to attract are those who are wary of the, as they see it, "hyped-up Americanism" of some of the other companies. They're interested in the MLM concept but they want a company with a good track record and a repeatable product range; something which is more . . . British.'

> *'How are the products sold?'*

'By the distribution of our catalogues, which you pick up the following evening. Being realistic, if you were just starting we would only expect that three out of ten would give you an order. If you go back in three months' time – because that's what it's all about, repeat business – you'll find that probably nine out of ten of the people who bought the last time will buy again. The average order value from a customer is about £8.50. One of my distributors will personally do £400 in business every single week for 21 hours' work. That's a lady with three children, and she'll do that 51 weeks of the year. Just distributing catalogues! I have sponsored a lecturer from Belfast, he and his wife have been with us for fourteen and a half years, they've got no agents, they've just been calling on the same customers for all those years.'

'Why do you state that there is no selling involved?'

'If a person says to me, "I thought there was no selling in this," I say to them, "If you go into a supermarket today and lift something off the shelf and pay for it, the girl at the checkout didn't sell it to you, did she?" The answer is no, of course. And it's the same with us, we're not using our skills or persuasion to get you to buy it, the customer has just looked at the catalogue and decided. I had an agent in the days before the catalogue, when we had a series of glossy pictures that we would show to people in their homes. She didn't sell a thing. When we went over to the catalogues I gave her a call to explain to her how much easier it was, and she came back into the business and is now doing well. She will tell anyone that although she markets £400 worth of products a week she does not regard herself as selling.

'If you look back at our history we are seen to be a company that goes and knocks on doors, and most people who know our name expect that they have got to go out and sell products. The catalogue is designed so that they do not have to do it. All you've got to do is to learn the skill of placing the catalogue, going back the next day and picking up the orders already done. We don't tell our people how to sell a product but we give them a cast-iron guaranteed way of doing it. If you get those catalogues in enough people's houses you *will* make money. If you put fifty out you will get 8, 9, 10 maybe 12 orders.'

'Do you ever get approached to join other companies' schemes?'

'We try to control this but it is a temptation for many people who have an organization and see a new product, and maybe a refinement to the plan that makes it look like they will make more money. We're truthful with what we say and we don't quote what anybody's earning because what impresses someone won't impress someone else. Earnings can be misleading but a lot of companies put a lot of gloss on it and try to impress people.'

'Why should anybody join Kleeneze rather than another company?'

'It's £18 to start, we've got a large guaranteed product range of things that most people need, most of the products are repeatable, you can offer your customer the facility of paying by credit card, which very few MLM companies do. If you do get a credit card order it is generally much higher than a cash order. You've got a very reliable delivery service and credit facilities for agents – you have actually got a week to pay for your order once it has been delivered.'

'*What's the most difficult part of the business for you?*'
'Trying to encourage and persuade and prove to people who have just joined the potential they have in running an MLM business with Kleeneze.'

'*If I had just joined up with the intention of building a big business, what should I be doing tomorrow?*'
'What I want you to do is sit down tonight and think of all the people that you know whom you think would welcome another income. Either arrange for them to come round to your house in a couple of nights' time and I'll come along and talk to them, or arrange for the two of us to go to their homes to talk to them without any obligation. You can actually do that right away, just as I did, but I did it off my own bat. I don't recommend any particular way of inviting people, it depends on your own personality. Just give them the facts, you've only just got involved in this business, you don't know all the answers yet but you know there's a lot of money to be earned. Would they come along, but stress that there's no obligation.'

'*What has been the biggest benefit to you in joining Kleeneze?*'
'Well, income certainly. Being my own boss and being able to organize my life the way I want it, being able to take holidays whenever I want. I've just come back from a month's holiday and my business was able to take over and do exceptionally well the month I was away. There's not many businesses where you can do that, you'd be worried sick about all sorts of things. Being able to travel the world and have financial independence.'

'*What sort of income can one expect at the top levels in Kleeneze?*'
'One of our managing distributors [6 or 7 personally-sponsored 22

per cent groups] makes about £45000 a year gross, and he does no selling whatsoever; he makes that on overrides.'

'What are your goals for your business?'

'I'm the third in the company at the moment, my goal is the top position eventually. I know exactly what I want and when I'm going to go for it, but I don't quote it.'

'Talking of MLM generally, what is the most important quality required for success?'

'Determination. The setbacks I've had, the setbacks the people I know have had . . . you get someone you think is really going well in the business and they suddenly have to stop for all sorts of reasons. You must be determined, all those little things that happen along the way, you have to keep keeping on. And you must be very well organized, if you're not, your business will just collapse. There are people who are very good at getting people, but once they get those people it all collapses because they just can't handle the bookwork. Empathy is very important. Some people are so self-centred that they just can't appreciate what the person they are talking to is looking for, so they fail to motivate them. You must also be able to talk to all levels of people in the business, you must not dismiss the smallest businesses in your organization. All those people make the business. All these things are component parts of being positive. Any business has its share of setbacks and problems, and if you're easily put off at the first hurdle, you're down.'

'What sort of training and motivation do you give your group?'

'I do a regular bulletin, and I run competitions to motivate them to sponsor. We have house meetings rather than meeting in hotels. Twice a year we might all have a dinner in a hotel, but we find we get a better response with the informal atmosphere. Perhaps one person will stand up and relate how they were successful last week, or how well they distributed their catalogues. Or we'll have a very young fellow who has sponsored a lot of people telling some of the older people who haven't sponsored anybody how he did it.'

'What about business aids?'

'The company do just these two tapes [audio and video]. When you or your group have done £200 in a month for the first time you get the video, a business presentation portfolio, a company tie or scarf, pen and 100 "Air Miles". This is a business development aid, you've shown that you have a flair for the business and this is to help you sponsor more people.'

'How much do you sell every month?'

'Nothing. The first week in the business fifteen years ago I set up three agents and then went out and advertised for agents. When I first got my kit I realized it wasn't just about selling, it was about building up a team. I'm not interested in that part of the business. I would never have been in the business today if I'd had to go door to door. A person can come into our business and do wholly selling if they wish, or they can do selling and sponsoring, or they can do no selling at all if they so wish; you don't need to in order to make money.'

'But if everybody sponsored people but did no selling nobody would make any money.'

'We must be practical about it, we all know that however good the opportunity is or how good the company is there will be people who will not be capable of doing that, people who won't understand it, people who just won't do it. That means that those who do do it have got great prospects. If you take a hundred people, human nature being what it is, there is always a percentage who will never, never, never build a business, no matter what you tell them. Because of Kleeneze's extensive product range, with many items being repeatable, you only need each of your agents to have a small number of customers to have a regular income from the whole group.'

'Do you have a retirement option in the plan?'

'No. You have to keep your personal group volume at the 17 per cent level to qualify for bonuses, so you have to keep on sponsoring. The only retirement option is that if anybody wants to they can offer to sell their business to the company at a privately negotiated rate, there isn't a set figure. There are a lot of people in our business who would carry on after 65. There's a man in Scotland who's getting a very good income from his group and he's over 70.'

Judith and Cyril Leedham

Judith (44) and Cyril (48) have lived in the same house for twenty years, in a small village near Uttoxeter. They have always been in retail businesses of one kind or another which have been successful enough to keep them reasonably well off. They have not had a mortgage for eighteen years and have always had the benefit of two cars and a caravan. They are 'Executives' with the Uni-Vite company, which means that they have sponsored six people who have become 'Circle Leaders' (their groups' monthly sales are over £1500). They reached this level in November 1986, having started their Uni-Vite business in September 1984. Judith started the business on her own and Cyril joined her in partnership some six months later, when Judith went full-time into the business, giving up her hairdressing salon. By August 1987 Cyril was also full-time with Uni-Vite. Their Uni-Vite business has more than comfortably replaced the income earned from their previous businesses.

'How did you get involved with MLM?'
Judith: 'I got involved by accident. My sister-in-law was a Uni-Vite advisor in Somerset, who suggested that I might like to try the products because she knew I was always interested in losing weight, and she came and brought me six tubs of diet drink mix. I said that there was no way I needed six of them but she said that she knew that if I started using them others would want them. Within three days the other five had been sold! I then enrolled as an advisor myself, and by January I was making more money than I was in the hairdressing salon, through retail sales and by having brought in two or three people. I finished the salon at the end of March and went full-time, converting the salon into an office and distribution centre for Uni-Vite. My husband had been behind me all the time and had been interested in it.'

'Where did you find your new advisors?'
'From people who were customers in the first instance. They would

be asking for six tubs for their friends at work and I would say that they should become advisors themselves, and it went on from there.'

'Were all your advisors originally customers?'
'I can honestly say that all our advisors were customers.'

'Is advertising a very effective way of getting new advisors?'
'No.'

'What is the most effective way?'
'Getting satisfied customers.'

'So when you started to build your business seriously your first job was to get new customers?'
'Yes. You could advertise for customers, obviously. Only well-looked-after customers make good advisors. If you don't look after your customers and show them, by example, how to be a good advisor, then of course they will not make a good advisor.'

'So how did you go about getting new customers?'
'We would advertise, do leaflet drops, I do all sorts of things, town-centre promotions, shows, exhibitions. Word of mouth recommendation is always the best advertising and the cheapest, it cannot be beaten. I am not a great fan of advertising, I always say to people advertising is your last resort, not your first. A satisfied customer will always bring in four or five more. A dissatisfied customer will lose you ten. MLM grows by talking. I talk to anyone, anywhere about Uni-Vite, it has become a way of life to us.'

'What have been the greatest benefits to you of having a good MLM business?'
'I think job satisfaction, we enjoy it. We've met loads of people we wouldn't otherwise have met, been to loads of places that we wouldn't otherwise have been to. We have always been in business, but MLM has tremendously enriched our business knowledge.'

*'If someone has an interest in diet products and food
supplements, and has decided that they want to get
involved in MLM, why do you think they should consider
Uni-Vite?'*

'Because it's British-run by the four original owner-directors. It's a
British product developed in Britain, and we have a friendly
atmosphere between all of our people. The back-up is there, also we
have our own executive association where we all get together
without the company and discuss the company, and let them know
what we think. There's a continuous development in the diet and
nutrition field, like the new "Mind and Body" programme which
teaches the mental aspect of dieting. There is a continuous
progression of the company. The great thing with Uni-Vite is that
it's not just selling a product, it's helping others as well. If someone's
going on a diet it is usually a minimum of three to four weeks, so
you're going to meet them three to six times. Another thing is that
every advisor deals direct with the company and is supplied direct by
the company with products and commission cheques.'

'What's wrong with American companies?'

'I think British firms are well run, we haven't quite got the hype of
some of the American companies. British companies are more
down to earth, and suit the British nature. Six weeks before I was
offered Uni-Vite I had been put off MLM by the way I was offered
a business with an American company. It was this "Come round,
I've got a business you just can't refuse to join" invitation. When the
guy doing the presentation heard that we had our holidays in a
caravan he said, "You don't want to have caravan holidays for the
rest of your life, do you? Don't you want to go abroad?" I said that
I had been abroad but that I happened to prefer my caravan! Uni-
Vite was much more upfront – "this is it, this is the product" – you
had to use the product before you became an advisor anyway.'

*'How do you split the work between yourself and your
husband?'*

'We both work full-time in the business, we do most of it together.'

'What are a sponsor's main responsibilities, in your view?'

'New people must know that they can come to their upline for help, guidance and support. I think a lot of MLM people don't realize sufficiently their responsibility to the people they bring in. There are a lot of people who come into MLM who, unlike ourselves, have not been in business before, and their upline do not teach them things like bookkeeping and the tax man. When you are self-employed and building your own business you have to realize that it can be up to two years before the tax man comes knocking on the door. It's very easy for a person who has not been self-employed before to run away with the idea that all the money they're earning is theirs.

'It's one of the more important things for a long-lasting business because I've seen a lot of people fall by the wayside, not because they lost faith in any product or company, but because they spent all the money that came in and eventually their tax debt was so much that they had to go and do something else. I've seen people have to sell their homes, I've seen marriages break up; people who were earning massive amounts of money and spending it all because they have not been taught how to handle money. I always teach my people that you put a third away for the tax man, you re-invest a third into the business, and a third is yours. At the end of the day you'll always have some savings left over from the tax man.'

'So what you're saying is to run it like a proper business from the start?'

'You've got to realize from the first day that, if you've gone into it correctly, this is going to build into a *business*, and a business has to be run on a businesslike footing. You must keep books, every expense must be recorded, because at the end of the day you are going to be accountable to the tax man. I would advise anyone to inform the tax man immediately of what they are doing.'

'How much do you sell personally per month?'

'In Uni-Vite you have to do a minimum of £150 retail sales yourself per month to qualify for commission, and your breakaway groups have to qualify every month. The commission structure is geared to motivate you to build your network "wide" as well as "deep".'

'What would you say to someone who was wondering whether to go into MLM?'

'They should go into it realizing that it is hard work. To make a full-time business of it you've got to be very committed, with the right product, and really stick at it. You have to put faith into it. One thing I disagree with is the hype which says that you can earn thousands and thousands with very little effort. I think people should beware of any company who's promising them massive incomes from sitting at home sending a few letters and mailshots out and expecting a business to grow. I think that what people have got to do is really check the company out, make sure it's not being run from somebody's front room. I think they should look very carefully into a company before they put a lot of their time and effort into it, and make sure that it is a feasible and stable company to join. I think that the product makes a big difference too; I remember a company that started MLM with groceries! It didn't last five minutes because there's hardly any profit margin on groceries, and because to send off an order every week with a cheque for your groceries is not what people want to do. A successful MLM company has to have a novelty product.'

'A novelty *product?'*

'Yes, a novelty product. It has to be something that people want, that's usable, consumable ...'

'But does that necessarily mean a novelty product?'

'What I mean is that they have to have a product which people can't pick up off the shelf in the supermarket.'

'What would you say is the one main key to success in MLM?'

'Helping others to achieve what they want. If you don't involve other people and help them to get what they want, you don't get what you want. It all comes back to looking after the people you bring in.'

Brian and Barbara Jacques

Brian and Barbara live in the nicest part of the market town of

Leighton Buzzard in a five-bedroomed house with three offices and an indoor swimming pool. There is a Mercedes in the drive, two other cars having been disposed of because they only ever drove one of them at a time. They have two daughters and a son, all adults, and have been with Shaklee (UK) Ltd (now part of Nature's Sunshine Products) for fifteen years, having been at the highest level – 'Master Coordinator' – for eleven of those years. Barbara had previous experience in direct sales, working with the Tupperware corporation, and prior to that with Spirella, the corset company. Brian's advice remains sound and relevant, regardless of the demise of Shaklee in the UK. His story, like those of all successful distributors, is fascinating.

'How did you get into multi-level marketing?'

'It must be twenty years ago, we started off with one of the pyramid companies, Holiday Magic, although we didn't operate it that way. We always sold the products, you see, but the idea really was that you were supposed to sell people a position within the structure by getting them to "buy in", the selling of the products being of secondary importance. None of our people bought a position at all, and we had quite a large organization with all our people working their way in. Other people in the company weren't interested in the products at all, they were solely interested in finding others to invest £1000 in stock. The company started to bring in even more people who were great exponents of this "buying in" and I didn't like the look of it at all because they were even encouraging people to remortgage their houses to get some money to join up. I got out at that point.'

'What happened after you left?'

'I started a mortgage broking business which was quite successful for two or three years, which I sold in the end. Then I started a used car business which I had for a few years, after which I had a spell as a greeting cards salesman. The card firm then made me redundant; I went very briefly into local government, didn't like the look of it – no competition there! – and got out of it. That took me to 1975 when we started with Shaklee. We knew their sales manager at that time and she sponsored us into the company.'

'How did you get your new Shaklee business off to a good start?'

'We approached people that we knew. We had always held the rank of "Supervisor" because we qualified in the first month by a combination of personal and group sales. Some of the people we got together with in small meetings, others we went to see individually. We only signed up four people in that first month, and we did a "PV" [a value assigned to each product] of £1383, Supervisor level being £1200. Good going when you consider that a lipstick was only 60 pence! The next month we did £2500, and the third month in the business we did £4006 and broke out two first-level Supervisors. Nine months later we had the very first "bonus" car from the company.'

'What were you mainly selling at that time?'

'Skin care and cosmetics. We didn't have nutrition products at that time.'

'How long did it take you to get to Master Coordinator level?'

'Four years from start.'

'How hard did you have to work to do that?'

'Very hard. We each put twenty hours a week into it. At the time we both had full-time jobs, but within a few months Barbara gave up hers to devote more time to the business. Almost two years later I went into it full-time.'

'Did your children follow you into MLM?'

'There's three of them, and it's interesting that our eldest daughter made Master Coordinator, had a car from the company and travelled the world with us too. The middle daughter also had a free car through her Shaklee business, and we have a son who was also a Coordinator, and he had a bonus car too.'

'What would be the most effective way to build a business?'

'You initially trawl around your friends, your family and your relatives, that's the most efficient way of doing it. They are people that you know and you can practise on them, and if you muck it up you can always go back again later and have another go. You put everyone you know on the prospect list and start working through the list. Once you get very proficient at it you can go back to the ones where you mucked up and have another go!'

'Should you concentrate on sponsoring or selling?'
'Initially you have to do both because the selling makes you a bit of money. Bringing the people in then starts to develop the group, because, after all, you're very limited with what you can do yourself in the time that's available, bearing in mind that most people work at it part-time. In doing this you've got to make sure that the hours are worked effectively. It's no good swanning off and selling a pile of products if you're not developing the group because you're not going to get very far and it's going to be damned hard work as well.'

'What advice would you give to someone who likes the concept of MLM and wants to pick a good company to start with?'
'First and foremost you have to research the company. That is what we did when we joined Shaklee. Research the company, find out who owns it, find out what they're doing, what the turnover is, probably try to meet some of the people – particularly those who run the company. The financial position of the company is important, so have a look at their annual report. You can't run a company on a shoestring because it isn't going to survive. You need a company that has stability and a good product range, and who is a leader in their particular field. Finally, they have to be members of the Direct Selling Association. If they are none of those things, forget them.'

'Why should someone get into MLM as opposed to some other type of business, say a franchise?'
'MLM is one of the most effective ways of getting the product to the consumer with minimal capital outlay to yourself, and if you get with a good company you'll get the maximum reward for doing it. If you go into a franchise you have to put money up, a franchise fee, premises, stock and all the rest of it. Unless you're prepared to do that sort of thing then it's not for you, because you haven't got the resources to get into it. MLM is one of the best ways for most people

because you can get into most schemes for virtually nothing, and the rewards are substantial if you're any good at it.'

'What makes a person successful in MLM?'

'Dedication to it. Dedication, interest and patience. You need a lot of patience in the beginning. The basic problem is that a lot of the people who come into it look at it like a job, and expect to get a wage at the end of the month. Of course it doesn't work that way, you have to give it time to build up. There's an old MLM saying that in the beginning you do a lot of work that you don't get paid for, and later on you get paid for a lot of work you don't do. You have to look at it with a long-term view, which is why you need a company which is stable.'

'What are the merits, or otherwise, of advertising for distributors?'

'The problem is that it can be very expensive and very frustrating. You don't know what you are going to get out of it; we reckon that if you get one person out of an advertisement you've done pretty well. We've had nothing at all from some advertisements we've run. We are consistent in our advertising, and where a lot of people tend to advertise locally, we always advertised nationally, when we had built up the funds to do so.'

'What sort of wording would you use in such an advertisement?'

'Something like: "Ever thought about making money but wondered where to start? We are part of a large international corporation specializing in nutritional products etc. Good earning potential together with bonus car scheme, conventions, retirement programme possible. Write for details.' We've developed quite a few of our supervisors out of that sort of advertisement. We used to run it regularly, for several years in fact. We get through an awful lot of people to find some good ones. One of the basic problems is that people who do advertising are looking for "distributors", and, frankly, that's all they get. When we are advertising we are looking for Coordinators or supervisors at least. In other words, what you look for is what you get. If you look for distributors, that's what you find; if you look for Coordinators, that's what you find. We always ask our people, "When you go out recruiting, what are you looking for?" They say, "Oh we're looking for distributors," and we say, "Well that's all you'll ever get." We look for Coordinators and that's why we get the Coordinators. You get what you look for, it's as simple as that.'

> *'What do you do when you get answers to your*
> *advertisements from all over the country?'*

'If we have one of our group in the area we will pass the information to them to deal with. If the enquiry is from a new area I will do that myself.'

> *'However far away they are?'*

'Yes, however far away. I always have people write to me, so at least you know they are reasonably keen. I will then telephone them, tell them about it and how we got involved and make an appointment to go and see them. I will tell them that I am going to send them some literature to study before I meet them, to get them acquainted with the products and the company. A day or two before going to see them I will ring them again to confirm the appointment. At that point they have the opportunity, if they don't like the look of it, to cancel the meeting and save me a journey. If they like what they see and start to ask me questions I'll ask them to keep their questions until I see them, when I will run through the whole programme with them. One thing I never do is argue with someone to try to change their mind. If they decide they don't want to do it, that's fine by me, goodbye, finish. I might say to them that I feel it's a shame because I think they would be pretty good in this sort of business, but that's all I would say. If you've got to start convincing somebody from the very start, you're going to have trouble with them for the next ten years.'

'How do you and Barbara split the work between yourselves?'
'It's always me who goes out doing the recruiting, I'm the best recruiter in the world, I could get two out of three in! Then Barbara would follow up with the product training. We're the best team in the world!'

'What has your MLM business brought you that you wouldn't have otherwise had?'

'It's made us a lot of money, for sure, there's little question about that, although we've ploughed a lot back into the business. We've had the nice cars out of it, and we've travelled the world. And good health is probably the biggest benefit of all. Plus of course we've been able to help a lot of people along the way.'

'Any final comments?'

'You've got to be patient, you've got to get your act together, you've got to devote time to it, and if you really want to do well and get to the very top you've got to plough some of those bonus cheques back into it. Sometimes you'll be out there every evening of the week and you'll be so damned tired you'll wonder what the hell it's all about, and the following morning you'll have to get up and go to work. But it's worth it!'

9: Myths and Misunderstandings

This chapter will tell you how to answer the most common questions and criticisms of the MLM concept confidently, including:

- pyramids;
- saturation;
- cults;
- the 'ground floor';
- getting people to sell for you;
- the small percentage that succeed;
- using people;
- getting hassled to sell;
- losing money.

Multi-level marketing is significant in the economy of many countries, but because of its chequered history and its uniqueness as a form of marketing products it is probably the least understood and most *mis*understood business. Once you get involved in it you will encounter all types of response from people, most of whom will have no background of factual knowledge of the subject. This chapter will help you to parry the inevitable but awkward questions about MLM which an uninformed majority will ask with irritating regularity. Many of the clichéd statements you will encounter are discussed in some detail. If you can face the challenge of this type of question and respond with authority, conviction and enthusiasm, you will not only be doing your part to assist in raising the public profile of MLM to where it belongs, but you should also find your business benefitting from it.

The discussions below are meant to assist you whenever the phrases are repeated. My advice on dealing with people who are intent on criticizing MLM with unfounded and unsupportable statements, and with those who are merely misguided, is to dissect their arguments and ask for an explanation of what is meant by each part. You should then be able to put the facts right easily (with the help of this chapter), and permanently educate them on this important but very misunderstood business. Let's start with the 'classic'.

'It's pyramid selling'

Where do you start with this one? How about a definition: the *Oxford English Dictionary* defines 'pyramid selling' as 'a form of financial trickery', which is exactly what it was. I say 'was' because pyramid selling as described in the following paragraphs no longer legally exists. The confusion which arises is caused by naming all forms of multi-level marketing as 'pyramid selling'. If people wish to do this, fine, but they should be aware of the difference between illegal, undesirable schemes and legal, ethical schemes. Unfortunately, the phrase is often used by people who do not even know what pyramid selling or genuine multi-level marketing are. It is brought out at the first mention of bringing others into the business, as if such an aspect is inherently objectionable. Let's have some facts here: are there any large businesses or organizations which do not have a pyramidal structure? None that I know of. They all have a big chief at the apex who has recruited several executives to help him develop a large profitable organization consisting of numerous levels of employees. Every marketing structure for every type of product consists of several levels of distribution (wholesaler, retailer, and so on) with each level making a profit of a percentage of the final retail price, depending on the amount of product they can turn over.

To be fair to your questioner, true pyramid selling caused such a public menace up until the time of its cessation (by means of the Fair Trading Act 1973) that it is hardly surprising that so many people have a mental block concerning anything remotely similar. The fact is that the basic concept behind pyramid selling was, and still is, logical, successful and attractive. Like any good idea, the concept can be abused in the hands of the unscrupulous, and this is what happened with the 'pyramids'. 'Entry fees' of large sums of money were demanded of the prospective participants in some schemes, with promises of recouping this and profiting further by the introduction of more participants. The products in many cases were secondary to the operation of the scheme (or, rather, scam) and were often of dubious quality. Before seeking any orders from customers, participants were encouraged to purchase stocks of goods for distribution to future participants, the larger the quantity the larger the discount, and the greater the profit when sold on to the next recruits.

The corruption of an otherwise sound marketing concept was the encouragement to attempt a short cut to success – an impossibility in any proper business. The practice became known as 'front end loading'. Hard luck on anyone who detached themselves for a moment from the excitement of promises of future wealth and decided that it was not such a good idea after all. The only way they were going to rid themselves of the stocks of product and recoup their initial investment was to recruit further people and/or try to sell the products as best they could. This of course was perfectly possible, but it required a certain ruthlessness to perpetuate a trading scheme which you had already decided was suspect. Even if the goods involved were of saleable quality, the totally negative motivation ('if I don't sell this lot it's money down the drain') is not the ideal way to conduct a successful direct selling business.

The 'multi-level' concept can be a very powerful method of moving products and building a profitable business. People exposed to it for the first time, especially in the highly-charged atmosphere of excitement which was created in the 'pyramid' presentations, often threw their normal caution to the wind, convinced that great wealth was easily obtainable. While still in this excited state many people parted with significant sums, sometimes even being encouraged to remortgage their houses, to join the schemes and purchase goods. It was only later, when they had come down to earth, that the reality sank in. And the reality was that recruiting people into anything is not easy, especially if you no longer believe in the cause. If the products involved were worthless the task became more difficult still.

Parliament finally stepped in and passed regulations governing the operation of all 'multi-level' schemes in 1973. The regulations outlawed the objectionable aspects of the pyramid schemes, creating criminal offences against promoters and participants who attempted to continue them or start up new ones. (It should be remembered that before, during and after the time that the 'pyramid' problem was at its worst there *were* genuine companies with genuine people operating genuine schemes, many of which are still around and more successful than ever.)

Now back to your questioner: how do you respond? I suggest you reply with, 'What's pyramid selling?' and see what answer you get. What is most likely is a very vague and uninformed statement bearing no relationship to the scheme of which you are part or to which you are referring. You are then able to reply with, 'Well *this* isn't pyramid selling then.' Or you may get a slightly more accurate assessment, although still with an undertone that the business method itself is somewhat suspect. Your ideal response to this is something like, 'yes, that's basically how this business works, but you seem to think that there's something wrong with it.' Let them explain themselves precisely until they realize that there is no more reason for suspicion of the concept of multi-level marketing than for any other business. Of course you may not get this far with someone who is not open-minded enough to be proved wrong.

It really is time that the phrase 'pyramid selling' was put to rest for good, as it does not have any function other than to cloud the issue of the legality and integrity of genuine multi-level marketing. Unfortunately, for the reputation of good MLM business, the new regulations covering such schemes (*see* Chapter 10) still refer to Part XI of the Fair Trading Act 1973 which describes MLM as pyramid selling. There is only one type of scheme that I can think of which can properly be described as a pyramid scheme and that is any scheme where the safeguards of the regulations governing MLM are contravened or craftily eluded, and large sums of money are required from participants for such benefits as instant promotion within the scheme or various 'services'. In one recent fraudulent operation a number of recruits paid to a company more than £10000 each, after seeing some very impressive mathematics relating to their probable earnings in the scheme. This payment was for the dubious privilege of becoming one of a restricted number of initial distributors who would then receive a 'service' – the printing and distribution of thousands of leaflets which were supposed to be effective in sponsoring hundreds of new people into the business. Naturally, the leaflets did nothing of the sort, and the unfortunate investors had little chance of recouping their money.

I should also mention here that many people apply the term 'pyramid selling' to what I would describe as a chain letter. These are fully explained in Chapter 3; they are in fact another version of the multi-level concept, but one without any genuine product involved. The 'product' is usually a series of worthless photocopied reports, which are provided to participants to make it seem as though they are actually buying something for their £5. The schemes really are nothing but a method of circulating money. They are not true pyramid schemes in that there is no risk of losing a great deal of money by being stuck with large amounts of unsaleable products, although many people have spent much time, and incurred costs of £100 or more buying mailing lists and addressing envelopes to hundreds of people. Contrary to the exaggerated claims in the literature, surveys have not revealed anyone who has made a significant amount of money from participating in such a scheme.

'It'll saturate'

Someone once said, 'You can prove anything with statistics.' I would add that you can prove anything with mathematics, especially that an MLM scheme can 'saturate' (whatever that means) in as short a time as you like. Time for another *OED* definition. 'Saturation point' is 'that beyond which no more can be absorbed or accepted'. So saturation, in MLM terms, means that there are no more people around to sponsor or to whom you can sell products. Can this actually happen? We will see, but first some mathematics to 'prove' that it can.

Imagine a brand-new MLM company starting up and sponsoring three people to get things rolling. I am going to assume that each person sponsors three further people within one month and then stops sponsoring. Therefore in month one there are twelve $(3 + 3^2)$ distributors. By month two there are 39 $(3 + 3^2 + 3^3)$ distributors. Following this logic, by the twelfth month there will be 2 391 483 distributors. Remember we have not even considered customers yet. By the end of two years the distributor force has risen to more than 1 270 887 000 000 – 250 times the population of the world.

There you have it – proof that all schemes will saturate after a very short period of time, making it a waste of anyone's time even to think of getting involved. But hang on a minute, if all schemes are supposed to fizzle out within a couple of years at most, how come there are a number of companies who have been operating their systems for many more years than that, even decades? There you have your first answer to the fallacy of saturation. No company would continue to expand after their first two years if it were true. The facts of the matter could not be further away from the description 'saturation'. Few of the largest and longest-running companies in the UK have an active distributor force approaching 100,000 let alone millions, so the facts dispose of the mathematics with ease. But why are the true distributor figures so low in comparison to the figures obtained by simple mathematics?

Every person is different. This obvious statement is not considered in the calculations above. The difference that this would make is that you cannot get a situation where *every* distributor sponsors at the rate of even three per month. In real life what happens is that a hard-working distributor who manages to sponsor three others within a month will be disappointed to find that probably two of them will have dropped out within another month. If he continues to work hard and sponsor another three the next month he will find, human nature being what it is, that again he soon has only one of these left the following month. He will be lucky if he finds that one of his two remaining distributors decides to take the business seriously and begins to sponsor people himself. You can see now the kind of persistence that is necessary to build a big MLM business, to sift through enough people to find that half-dozen or so who are committed to making it work. You can now also see how ludicrous it is to pretend that it can grow as fast as the figures I quote above.

The population of any country, and of the world, is dynamic. That is to say that it looks different at every point in time when you examine it. The number of births each year in the UK is probably in the region of five hundred thousand. If you consider that the increase in the number of active distributors in any one year in the average MLM company is likely to be far less than 10000 you can see that there is absolutely no chance that there will be nobody left to sponsor at any time.

A simple piece of market research would prove that saturation is not feasible. If you were to ask a hundred people at random if they know anything about multi-level marketing, my experience is that around eighty of them will not even have heard of it, and another ten will think they know about it but will not understand it properly. 80 per cent of the population will be seeing something totally new if you present the MLM opportunity to them. The next ten per cent would start to understand the business better on having it explained properly. The remaining ten per cent will either be distributors themselves or be uninterested in MLM. Wouldn't anybody agree now that there is virtually unlimited opportunity to develop MLM for many decades without 'saturation' becoming the remotest possibility?

How would you tell when saturation occurred anyway? When there is not one person left in the town/county/country/world who is interested in increasing their income? When there is nobody who would be interested in buying any of your quality goods? You might just as well say that J Sainsbury shouldn't bother opening any more stores because everybody buys food from somewhere already, so where are the new customers going to come from?

Not convinced yet? Accept for a moment that saturation hasn't happened yet (which you must agree is true), but that it will in the future. When will it occur? In five years? Ten years? Fifteen years? Whichever time period you choose, *you* have ample time to build a successful MLM business to whatever level you desire.

I do not believe that saturation can occur in *any* form of business, whether with regard to customers for a particular product or recruits for a particular activity. There is always a certain percentage of people who will be willing to participate in a specific activity. Your task in MLM is to find some of that percentage of the population who are looking for an opportunity like it.

'It's a cult'

Alternatively, 'It's a religion' or 'You'll be brainwashed.' This is an interesting one which we can examine in some detail. The *OED* calls a cult 'devotion or homage to person or thing (esp. derogatory of transient fad)'. Having read this far, you must accept that MLM is not a 'transient fad'. I accept that the general use of the word 'cult' is almost entirely derogatory, and the critic of MLM using the 'cult' phrase is not entirely wrong in suggesting that there is some 'devotion' to a 'thing', but should MLM be referred to in these terms?

You now know of the tremendous opportunity which is offered by MLM. You may find it quite exciting yourself to realize that you have exactly the same opportunity as everyone else to become as wealthy as you wish, if you are prepared to put forth the necessary effort into the business. Imagine the excitement generated within a person who has looked for a long time for the sort of opening that MLM offers, but who had almost given up hope of finding anything. The level of enthusiasm and commitment shown by such a person can be almost overpowering. Although enthusiasm and commitment are prerequisites of a highly successful MLM business, there is no need to become extroverted in order to activate these qualities. Like any person with a new time-consuming hobby, some distributors become so wrapped up in the development of the potential of their new business that, for a while, nothing else matters. In a case like this, then, you do have a cult, a 'devotion to a thing'. Naturally, anybody having been subjected to such enthusiasm *unwillingly* will recall the whole experience negatively and tar with the same brush all MLM business people. It is easy to take the view, without knowing the reasons for a person's newly-found excitement, that he has become this way because of some sinister action on the part of the MLM company involved or their distributors – 'brainwashing'?

Brainwashing is sinister, isn't it? It is the systematic replacement of established ideas in a person's mind by new ones. What is really sinister is what the established ideas in some people's minds actually are. Our minds are continually bombarded with bad news (how often is the news good?) and bad examples on television of how not to run your life. This is brainwashing at its worst. I am not advocating complete withdrawal from the facts and realities of life, but I am convinced that if people in general 'brainwashed' themselves with more positive thoughts more often, the world would be a better place to live. If your over-the-top MLM person *has* been brainwashed, by himself or by others, it will be with hope, determination and achievement, all thoroughly positive values. Can we not forgive his occasional excesses?

What about the 'religion' angle? This is based on the fact that MLM companies and large distributor organizations, like any big company which employs salespeople, regularly arrange meetings, seminars, rallies and conventions for the purpose of training, informing and motivating their people. Perhaps they are a bit like the religious conventions on an American preacher's tour. No doubt if you attended a sales convention where the company name was not displayed you would have some trouble deciding whether or not it was an MLM function (why don't conventional companies get the 'religion' tag?). These meetings are fun! The speakers are usually good, and always motivating. The audiences are happy, receiving information and motivation which will be profitable for them, so they will cheer and enjoy the presentation of awards on stage. Is this religion?

While on the subject of religion I might add that it has often been quoted that MLM companies, or some of them at least, are in fact evangelical religious movements. Fairly recently a 'quality' Sunday newspaper published an article about a possible takeover bid by Amway Corporation, one of the largest MLM companies in the world, for Avon Products, another company in the direct selling field. The paper quoted an American sociologist as saying that Amway '. . . is a religiously sectarian social movement'. The article also said that the company 'is said to indoctrinate its recruits in its evangelical free-enterprise beliefs'.

It is worth examining this closely, to get some facts straight. Were those who made these statements speaking from experience of being involved in the company themselves? I think we can assume that their information was second-hand, either from a practising or a resigned distributor. We can be sure that it was not the former, because the fact is that the company does not pursue, recommend or force any religious beliefs upon anyone, least of all their distributors. This is simple enough to confirm by asking any of them. The directors may have strong beliefs, but if you think about it you will agree that it would be commercial suicide even to attempt to promulgate them in any way. The distributor force of MLM companies is a cross-section of the population, just as the employees of any large company or organization are, and therefore contains the same percentage of strongly religious people as does the country as a whole.

Remembering that a company's distributors are all independent business people, it is not hard to imagine that once in a while one of them will decide to try to use the 'comradeship' of their own group as a means of expounding certain beliefs to them. This has happened in the past with Amway, and no doubt with other companies. What Amway did was promptly to issue a warning to all distributors against such conduct, threatening termination of any offending distributorships. A 'religiously sectarian' organization would not do this. The sociologist's information almost certainly has come from a resigned distributor. Many people resign from MLM distributorships because they realize that their desires are not strong enough to take them through the effort and persistence that are necessary to create a very profitable MLM business. This can give rise to a feeling of inadequacy or failure instead of realization and acceptance of limited financial ambitions. The comments of such a person about aspects of MLM generally, or a particular company, can often be tainted with exaggerations and put-downs in order to hide the truth of that person's resignation.

As for 'social movement', MLM companies certainly are this! They consist of people with goals and ambitions to improve themselves and their lifestyles by helping others to do the same – very social! Although this part of the statement was obviously meant to be part of the general criticism, perhaps it is more of a compliment.

The second statement from the article admits to being hearsay. 'Evangelical' is to do with 'spreading the gospel' (literally). You would certainly expect any company which is able to profit in a free-enterprise democracy, in contrast to the impossibility of its existence in another form of government, to believe fervently in this type of economy. Such a company is likely to inform its distributors, all of whom are profiting to a greater or lesser extent from their own enterprise, that free enterprise is 'a good thing'. Perhaps you could call this 'indoctrination'. MLM companies distribute products, not religion; they want to attract distributors, not lose them.

MLM is just business. But it is an exciting business. Its successful practitioners are generally happy, ambitious individuals who know where they are going in their business and their life, and who seek motivation and inspiration to help them realize their goals. In this respect they are unconventional people who will always inspire suspicion and bigotry in the minds of many of the majority.

'You have to be in at the start to make any money' or 'It's a ground-floor opportunity'

These are two variations on the same theme, a tricky one to discuss. In the 'business opportunities' section of the *Exchange and Mart* on any day there will be a number of advertisements offering opportunities with MLM companies, which give prominence to the benefits of the company being relatively new, and thereby being able to offer a 'genuine' ground-floor opportunity. A Department of Trade and Industry leaflet, *Multi-Level Selling Schemes*, gives this advice: 'A few people who get in right at the start might make extra money but don't let yourself be carried away by their success stories. The later entrants, at the bottom of the pyramid, may not do so well . . .' On the one hand, therefore, we have some MLM companies expounding the advantages of a system where those in first get the best deal, and on the other hand a government department advising people not to get involved in MLM due to the disadvantages of a system where only those in first can profit significantly. At least both parties appear to agree that the MLM concept gives the best chance of success to those 'at the top of the pyramid'.

How can I disagree with this consensus view? I have already stated that MLM offers an equal opportunity to everybody, and that you will earn what you are worth, and you will expect me now to justify those remarks. I would not want to write a popular book about a form of business in which only a few fortunate people can make any good money. I think the above-mentioned phrases constitute the most popular of all the misconceptions commonly held about MLM, for a number of reasons.

My first reason dervies from some simple logic. A company offering a ground-floor opportunity appears to me to be admitting that the good deal they are offering now will become less of a good deal as time goes on. When does it become a bad deal? When does a ground-floor scheme start becoming 'first-floor' or even 'second-floor'? If those who get in first get a better deal than those who get in later, there must come a point where it is not a good deal any more. If it is not a good deal any more, no one else will join and the whole thing will begin to collapse. This bears no relationship to what is happening in MLM today. Many older companies are steadily increasing their turnover year by year, despite the proliferation of new MLM companies in recent years.

One of the reasons that this 'get in first' fallacy has proved to be so popular is that it is based on a static mental picture of a pyramidal network structure, with one person at the top, perhaps three at the next level, nine at the next, and so on. The mental picture ends somewhere, maybe at the fifth level with 243 people, or the tenth level with 59040 people. At whichever level the picture stops there is a large number of people on that level who have no one in their organization, and who therefore cannot be making any more than a little retailing profit. Those at the top levels, however, are raking in the commissions from the sales of their considerable network. There is nothing wrong with this model of MLM except that it is static. It is a snapshot of the network at a particular point in time and takes no account of how these organizations are continually changing and growing. It is completely logical and acceptable that Fred, who started building his business two years ago, will be earning far more than Harry, who has only just begun. It also follows that in another two years, providing he works as hard as Fred, Harry will be earning a comparable sum to what Fred was earning two years ago. But by now, Fred has had another two years to build his business further, so Harry will not have caught him up on income level. As long as Fred and Harry both put the same amount of effort into their business, Fred will always be making more than Harry. However, they can both say, 'X years work gave me Y income.'

'Ground-floor' thinking fails to recognize the fact that, in a properly constructed marketing plan, you really do earn in direct proportion to your efforts. Nobody can get in at the beginning of a scheme and expect to become wealthy without putting in the requisite effort. Someone who joins a long-established MLM company today and works extremely hard will make far more money than someone who joins a brand-new company today and thinks that with a minimum of effort he will profit substantially because he is 'in on the ground floor'. There are hundreds of examples of people joining long-established companies, putting tremendous effort into the business and becoming those companies' wealthiest distributors. There are even more examples of people who joined MLM companies right at the beginning, did a minimum of work, and did not become wealthy at all. One MLM company director explained to me that when a company picks the right products at the right time and gets everything else right, they can experience 'explosive' growth in their organization; this means of course that many distributors' businesses become very profitable indeed. This argument, however, does not convince me that just because some people were there before the 'explosion' their particular businesses will increase dramatically without the required efforts on their part. Explosion or not, if two distributors in different places in a network are sponsoring new people at the same rate, then their organizations, and therefore their incomes, must grow at the same rate.

The 'ground-floor' advertisements may be placed by some companies and distributors simply because they realize that most people think they will be better off going with a brand-new outfit. If I have not won you around to my way of thinking on this subject, and you are determined to find a scheme where you can be in at the start, you had better make sure that your 'new' company is actually new. There are a number of examples of 'phoenix' companies which, for all sorts of reasons, failed initially. Some of these have risen from the ashes, hopefully with new and better managements and marketing plans, but maybe not. Whether a rehashed company can justifiably still call itself a ground-floor opportunity is a question you will have to answer yourself.

Another reason why the 'in at the start' fallacy is so widespread is that the first people to join an MLM company are often experienced multi-level marketers, who have already developed a large network of people willing to add another product or service to their portfolio. These people are able to show rapid growth of their business, and this is then put down to the fact that they were there first. The truth is that these people have already put in the effort required to build their business to that number of distributors, while the newcomer has to start from scratch. The newcomer, however, is at *no* disadvantage at all in starting late.

One aspect of MLM may affect your business depending on whether you join the company early in its life or much later – the products themselves. It must be a personal choice whether you prefer to deal with products that are completely new to the market or with products which have already established themselves with a good reputation. There are very few completely unique product lines in MLM; the business works best with products that have been shown to be in popular demand. A company whose distributors have, over a number of years, developed hundreds of thousands of customers all over the country, will be trusted and respected nationally. Because of the high turnover rates of direct sales people there are always many good customers around who have lost their distributor and are not sure how to find another one, so there are many ready-made customers for a well-established company's products. Finally, there is nothing to stop an older company continuing to bring out new products, which is exactly what does happen. A progressive company will be continually developing new products for its customers and distributors, any one of which could be the basis of a complete business.

'You have to get others to sell for you'

How many people are able to persuade others to go out and sell things for them? Would you sell for someone else? You cannot force people to do something they do not want to do. The only way to get people to do anything is to make it worthwhile and attractive for them. Conventional companies employ sales staff and give them the salary, commissions and other benefits to make it worthwhile for them. In MLM the only way that you can bring people into your network is to offer them the tremendous opportunity which attracted you in the first place. You will then find that you don't have to *get* them to do anything. They will be inspired by your sales efforts and they will sell because they realize that it will benefit them to do so, and because it will also inspire their own downline to sell. Here we are only considering MLM schemes in which selling to retail customers is an integral part of the business, but there are numerous schemes where there is no traditional selling, but rather regular purchasing by members of the network. In such a scheme there is no question of getting people out selling.

MLM people are there because they want to be part of it, not because someone else wants them to be. Without the necessary personal motivation they would not last long in the business. If they sell they are selling for themselves, nobody else. Naturally you will profit by your downline's sales, that's why you are in the business, but nobody ever grew rich (legally) without giving people what they wanted. You are giving people the chance that they may never have found alone. If you give people what they want you will always reap the benefits, and nowhere more so than in MLM. Your commissions could be compared to those obtained by recruitment agencies for finding good staff for companies, except that you are finding good people for your business at the same time as offering them their own.

'Such a small percentage ever make any money'

You may quite properly take this type of comment as an insult, as it takes no account of you and your decision to reach a certain level in your business. The phrase itself is one of those accurate but meaningless statements which can sometimes sound persuasive. You might just as well apply it to the population of the world, and it would be true again. The reason it is true is that only a small percentage of people are prepared to do what is necessary to become wealthy. The wealthiest people will tell you that they had no extraordinary talents or abilities which enabled them to get where they are. What they all did have, though, was a *burning desire* to succeed. This kept them going through all the setbacks and gave them the persistence to keep going until they got what they wanted.

Statistics can prove anything. For example, there are well over 50 million people in the UK and (if I am very fortunate) one in every thousand might have a copy of this book. Of those 50000 only one in a hundred will be reading it right now. That's 500 people out of 50 million, so the chance of *you* reading this book right now is only 0.001 per cent. That is patent nonsense of course, because you made the decision to start reading, so it was 100 per cent certain as far as you were concerned. When you make a commitment to yourself in MLM, or any other business for that matter, that you will do what it takes to get to the top, then you *are* going to get there. It is then

100 per cent certain that you will be one of the small percentage that make it.

'You'll lose all your friends'

When people say things like this, they mean that someone they knew (or a friend of a friend) got into MLM and became obsessed with it to the exclusion of everything else. They became a bore and a nuisance because everybody knew what was coming when they met them – insistence on them coming into the business or buying some product or other. The trouble with MLM is that it is so exciting some people cannot keep it in perspective, and they let it take over their life, even if only temporarily. Certainly, if you are to become very successful in MLM, you must be single-minded to an extent, but you must also give other people the amount of your attention they deserve; that is, attention to them as a *person* and not as a prospect or customer. Not everybody is going to feel the same way as you about the business, and if you disregard the views of others they will soon begin to disregard you. If you are to enjoy your success to the fullest you need to have balance in your life, a proper proportion of each constituent, and not overdo any part to the detriment of other important parts. This way you won't lose any friends.

As your MLM business grows you will grow as a person. You will learn to become a person to whom people are attracted, because it will profit you and because it is enjoyable. It is a fact of life that when a person develops he or she inevitably grows away from people who are not developing further, and this can include friends. This is not so much a case of losing friends but moving forward to newer ones more suited to your developing personality.

Another phrase you may hear is, 'My friend's marriage broke up when he got involved in that.' If you are one of a couple there is no guarantee that your partner will feel the same way about the MLM business as you do. This is often the hardest part of the business, as two people struggle to reach a compromise on a subject upon which they may have entirely opposing views. It is when compromises cannot be reached that relationships begin to suffer. Yes, marriages and friendships have broken up due to clashes of personalities triggered by one person's entry into an MLM scheme, but the MLM company or concept is not to blame. Any form of business or other interest can have the same effect if one person makes it too large a part of their life without taking full account of their obligations to others.

'The lower levels are exploited' or 'You're using people'

These comments are based on the idea that the large earnings of the top distributors come from the pockets of the lower levels. A few comparisons are in order here. Where do the earnings of your nine to five job come from? If you are employed by a company they will come from the company's profits, which come from the pockets of the buying public. Are the public being exploited by your company because of this? If you are a public servant your salary comes from the pockets of the ratepayers and taxpayers to whom you give an excellent service. Are they being exploited (no politics, please!)? Whatever products or services are involved in a business, a certain percentage is profit. The company makes the decisions as to where and how to apportion the profits, and in MLM a significant percentage of them are allocated to distributors in such a way as to reward them proportionately for the sales volume, and therefore profits, that their network produces. Does that sound like exploitation to you? I would call it performance-related payments.

A company could just as well decide to allocate their payments to sales staff dependent entirely upon the retail sales of the employee, as, of course, many companies do. In this way, although the sales staff are paid according to their efforts in selling, there is no motivation for them to find other good salespeople for the company. In this situation, sales personnel can probably earn more per sale than with MLM, but earnings are limited to a certain level. You can only sell so much per month on your own. In this method of doing business, staff are generally employed, so extra costs are incurred by companies in recruitment, motivation, training, administration, and so on. If, however, a part of that profit is put aside and shared out in such a way as to reward those who by their own efforts create sales networks of various sizes for the distribution of the company's products, then you have an MLM scheme with unlimited earning potential, and with all recruitment, training and motivation carried out by the distributors themselves. Every prospective distributor has a choice. He or she is provided with complete details of the company's marketing system and distributor rules which can be studied at leisure. A complete refund of every penny spent on starter kits and products can be had within seven days, or at least a 90 per cent refund after more than a week. This is *not* exploitation.

MLM people often get accused of 'using' people for their own benefit. Because success in MLM means finding other people who want the business too, this is often translated as using these people so that you gain whilst they somehow lose out. You should not forget that it is absolutely not the case that a distributor always makes more money than the people he or she sponsors. The person you sponsor may make a million, but you will only profit if you do your bit as well. 'Your bit' will depend on the exact rules of the company, but generally speaking you will have to work as hard as the person you sponsor in order to make the same amount of money.

Do you think a wealthy MLM distributor is going to say about his sponsor, 'He used me!'? Unlikely. All honest businesses profit only by giving others what they want. In MLM you are giving people a chance to change their life and lifestyle for the better, a chance that they may never have had before and but for you perhaps would never have got. You are doing them a favour – if they are not interested at least you have given them the opportunity.

What about the customers? Are they being exploited? If they are particularly gullible and you, by being particularly pushy, have sold them something they don't really want, then, yes, they have been exploited. I hope that this is not the way you would run your business. Ordinary people only continue to buy the same product because they like it and they consider it to be good value. There are hundreds of thousands, if not millions, of regular customers of products sold through MLM, creating sales in 1988 of more than £87 million in the UK alone. I believe this speaks for itself.

'I'll be hassled to sell, sell, sell'

Will you? Will you let somebody tell you how to run your business?

Will you allow yourself to be 'hassled to sell'? Of course you won't. If you sign up with a company and decide not to use or sell the products, that is entirely a decision for you. You will not earn any money doing this, of course, but it is up to you. It is your business. Even in the type of scheme which relies on personal use of products rather than retail sales, you will still have to sell the idea if you want to build a business. MLM *is* selling, like every other business. What is more likely to happen is that you will join the company of your choice and make a commitment to yourself to reach a certain financial goal, and you will ask your sponsor to help you. Until you abandon your goal or you quit the business your sponsor certainly will hassle you, and you will thank him for it when you reach your goal. This type of 'hassle' is of the most positive kind. Your sponsor will do everything possible to help you reach your goals because that will help him to reach his too. As soon as he gets a message from you that you do not want his help, he would be wasting his time to spend any more of it with you when it could be put to far greater use elsewhere.

The companies will give you every possible assistance and encouragement but certainly will not hassle you. They realize that it is only *you* who can make the commitment to become successful in building an organization to distribute their products, and that you are unlikely to do this if you feel pressured in any way.

'A friend of mine lost a lot of money in that'

'How, exactly?' is how you should respond to this one. There are only three ways of which I am aware that you can lose any money in MLM. The first usually applies to situations which occurred at least seventeen years ago, when there were no specific legal restraints upon MLM schemes, allowing 'pyramid' schemes to proliferate. The large investments that were sometimes required to enter these schemes could be lost. These amounts were recoupable, but only by persuading others to make the same sort of investment. Not everyone could do this, either because of a lack of persuasive skills or because of a conscience. Unfortunately, the Pyramid Selling Schemes Regulations are sometimes flagrantly ignored by fraudulent operators who, before they are detected and apprehended, are able to persuade numbers of people to part with large investments which they will not see again. The best advice, as always in MLM, is *never* pay any large sums of money to anyone for any reason other than to purchase previously ordered goods, if you want to be absolutely sure of staying clear of money problems.

The second way to lose money in MLM is to stockpile large quantities of products from a company which then folds, leaving you unable to return the goods for the refund to which you are entitled by law. They can of course still be sold to customers and other distributors, but this may not be as simple as it sounds. Product guarantees will become worthless and customers will certainly not be perfectly happy buying products from a non-existent company. The most common reason for this sort of stockpiling is that the distributor can immediately reach a higher level of discount, therefore providing higher profits than if products were only ordered in response to customer orders. Some companies do not allow this to happen, perhaps because of the risks, but also because they believe that no distributor should be able to gain that sort of advantage by having more money available than another distributor. The simple answer to whatever risks there may be in stockpiling is to refrain from doing it. It is not necessary or desirable. The motivation to sell and sponsor becomes negative when there is a large stock of products which need to be passed on *at all costs*. Any business person will tell you also that it is not good financial sense to stock any more goods than the absolute minimum, as it ties up money which could be put to far better use.

The only other way I know of losing money in MLM is to budget very badly and invest far too much money initially in sales and business aids such as leaflets, videos, business presentation equipment, advertising and other expenses. MLM nationally has a personnel turnover rate of 65 per cent (incidentally, far less than for participants in any other form of direct selling), so if a badly-organized distributor does not turn out to be one of the 35 per cent who do not quit the business, he will have a problem knowing what to do with his surplus items.

There you have three ways to lose money in MLM. None of them are due to a flaw in the concept itself, but rather to abuses of the concept or avoidable actions of participants. Before 1973 the concept could be abused to allow circumstances where losses could occur; after 1973 distributors could avoid any possibility of losses by exercising prudent business practices.

'You need to live in a densely populated area'

This phrase instantly identifies the critic as having only the sketchiest knowledge of the subject, usually obtained from a detractor of the business. It has been directed at me in the past, and is based on a couple of misconceptions. One is that unless the area in which you concentrate your business is densely populated, saturation will occur because all the customers of all of your downline will also live in the same area. The other is that you have to live fairly near the people you sponsor, presumably because of ease of distribution of the products.

For discussion in detail on the 'saturation' argument, *see* pages 189–91. You could be very wealthy indeed before the total number of customers of all of your downline reached the population of a medium-sized village. You know as well as I do that your customers do not have to come from the same street, town or county as you. It is obviously more convenient to be able to walk across the road to deliver a product to a customer, but there are plenty of ways of getting and supplying customers from all parts of the country. Many MLM companies deal with mail order goods exclusively, in which case it is irrelevant where your customer lives, even more so in a scheme where the distributors are the customers. It is possible, and quite common, for an MLM business to be administered entirely from home. Living near your downline (and upline) is certainly convenient, for product pick-up and also for being able to get together for meetings of various kinds, but it is by no means essential. Most companies have facilities for direct delivery of products to distributors who live a long way from their sponsors. Do not forget the international business available with many companies now – there is no need to live near people sponsored internationally.

'Aren't you liable for your group's losses?'

Your group cannot make any losses of the kind suggested by this question. You have already read above about the only ways of losing money in MLM. It is the responsibility of each person involved to manage their affairs in a sensible, businesslike fashion, and no one else can be held responsible for someone's failings in this regard. By budgeting properly and not spending unnecessary sums on excessive amounts of products, no one need ever be in a situation of financial loss in MLM. In any situation where losses are experienced, the last person who would be liable for them would be the sponsor or other upline of the person concerned.

'It's door to door!'

Well, so what if it is? There are actually very few companies who advocate selling door to door, as the method conjures up an unfavourable image of the brush salesman with his foot in the door. But I will reiterate: it is *your* business and you can run it how *you* like. There is at least one MLM company whose recommended method of selling is to place brochures of its products in a number of houses every week, either in person or through the letterbox, and pick them up in person a day or two later, at which time an order is sought. A perfectly good and, if professionally done, very effective way of selling.

Coleman Orr, a very successful MLM distributor from the USA, would forgive me, I am sure, if I repeated to you his way of responding to the above statement. 'Door to door's when you get up in the morning and go in the bathroom door, you brush your teeth and go in the kitchen door, eat breakfast and then get in the car door, slam, through the traffic, swear at all the other drivers, park at the factory, in the factory door where a buzzer tells you what to do all day, beep, in the canteen door, idle chatter, idle chatter, beep, back through the canteen door, work, work, beep, time to go home, get in the car door, through the rush hour, swear at the other drivers, get home, open the fridge door, get a beer, go in the dining room door, eat dinner, got in the TV room door, fall asleep on the couch, get up, go in the bathroom door, get washed, go in the bedroom door, go to sleep, get up in the morning and do it all over again. *That's* door to door, *and I don't do it*!' Nobody says 'door to door' to him any more.

Summary points

1. If they want to call it pyramid selling, fine, as long as they know what's legal and ethical and what isn't.
2. Don't worry about 'saturation', it can't happen.
3. If you want to get in 'on the ground floor' don't expect to be successful with less work than you would have to do if you got in at any other time.
4. You can be 100 per cent certain of being among the small percentage that 'make it'.
5. You can't lose money in MLM – if you're sensible with it.

10: MLM Law and Good Practice

This chapter will cover:

- the Fair Trading Act 1973;
- the Pyramid Selling Schemes Regulations 1989;
- trade descriptions;
- pricing;
- copyright;
- advertisements;
- ethical practices;
- the DSA Code of Practice.

Hopefully by now you will have come to the sensible conclusion that your multi-level marketing business needs to be conducted with the utmost honesty, integrity and professionalism if it is to grow unhindered by association with the problems and abuses of the concept which have occurred in the past. The MLM concept is still regarded with a great deal of unwarranted suspicion and narrow-mindedness by many people. However, it is steadily improving its position in the business world as more and more people realize its benefits, and new generations of young people grow up without preconceptions of, and prejudices against, the method. If this momentum is to be continued, for the benefit of your and everyone else's business, it is incumbent upon all MLM companies and their distributors to avoid situations which may generate bad publicity. This type of thing will turn back the clock with regard to the general public's perception of the MLM concept.

The diligent application of honesty and integrity in your business will serve you well and keep you out of any serious problems with your customers, your downline, and the authorities. This means making sure that you know as much as possible of the law and the ethics concerning the type of business you are in, and endeavouring to practise within the restraints imposed.

MLM companies can and must afford to engage experts and solicitors to pilot them carefully through the relevant legislation. New distributors cannot usually afford such a luxury. Although the companies have a duty to help distributors run their businesses correctly as well as profitably, and many of them do so admirably, they cannot be expected to fill their newsletters with the fine details of legislation. They would probably scare off more people than they recruited. This chapter is devoted to providing you with the information you will need to refer to from time to time to ensure that your business is conducted in a manner beyond reproach. Some of the following information is mainly applicable to the conduct and duties of the companies, but it has been included to allow you to be aware of what is legally required of the company with which you may be working.

The Fair Trading Act 1973, Part XI

Section 118   Contains a definition of the type of trading schemes which are controlled by the Act. The definition is necessarily complicated, comprehensive and virtually incomprehensible, and there is no benefit in going through it in detail here, other than to say that it covers virtually every type of MLM scheme, and most variations of the concept.

Section 119   Empowers the Secretary of State to make regulations governing the operation of such 'trading schemes' and the participants and promoters connected with them, which he did in the same year that the Act was passed. These regulations have now been superceded by the Pyramid Selling Schemes Regulations 1989 (*see* below) which came into effect on 1 March 1990, although contracts made between companies and distributors before this date are still effective.

Section 120   Defines a number of offences which may be committed by anyone involved in an MLM scheme if the provisions of the regulations are not followed or certain illegal payments are made or requested. The paragraphs concerning illegal payments are most important, as they contain the primary safeguard against the operation of a 'pyramid' scheme. The provisions deal with the most objectionable aspect of such a scheme, namely the 'investment' or 'entry fee' required for entry into the schemes. People were persuaded to make these payments because they were promised substantial returns by means of similar payments to them from new entrants whom they were able to recruit into the scheme. In this type of scheme the sale of products to retail customers became superfluous to the main aim of extracting sums of money from people. As you will know by now, in the most genuine MLM operations the sponsoring of a new distributor does not confer any benefit upon the sponsor, *unless* they are able to help the new distributor develop a successful business of retail sales of quality products to satisfied customers.

The section says that it is a criminal offence for anyone to request or accept any payment from a participant, or a prospective participant, of an MLM scheme if *a substantial part* of the inducement to make the payment is the prospect of receiving payments or other benefits solely in respect of the *introduction* of new participants.

Section 122   Lays down the maximum penalties to which offenders of the Act are liable – £2000 fine and/or 3 months' imprisonment if convicted in a magistrates' court, and an unlimited fine and/or two years' imprisonment if convicted in a crown court. The problems of pyramid selling schemes were not dealt with lightly. The government at the time was determined to stamp out the fraudulent operations and made sure that the penalties were a deterrent.

The Pyramid Selling Schemes Regulations 1989

These regulations lay down in detail the obligations of companies and distributors in respect of: contracts between the two parties; payments for goods and other items; advertising; information to be given on certain documents; distributors' rights.

During the very extensive consultation period associated with the drafting of these regulations the Department of Trade and Industry received many requests for a change of title, away from the phrase 'pyramid selling', which is associated by so many people with illegal schemes. It appears that the DTI expressed some sympathy with these requests, but felt that their hands were tied by the fact that the Fair Trading Act itself contained the phrase in the title to Part XI. To change a part of the Act would require action by parliament, a very long-winded procedure not justified by the size of the benefits accrued in the change of wording.

Regulation 4   Prescribes the information which must be included on any document intended to promote recruitment which indicates any financial benefits which may be obtained, except for advertisements in newspapers and magazines and documents handed out in public places. It was considered that there are suitable and sufficient statutory requirements and voluntary codes already in existence to deal with any problems arising from misleading or deceptive advertisements (*see* later comments on the Advertising Standards Authority's codes of practice). This regulation will therefore include mailshots, invitations to meetings, prospectuses and other literature available to prospects at meetings or personally handed to an acquaintance, but *only* if they contain any indication of possible earnings.

The information required in any such documents is as follows:

1. The date, or proposed date, of first operation of the scheme in the UK. Whether or not this information is actually useful, it can unfortunately also be misleading when applied to a scheme which has been restarted in a slightly different guise after perhaps being unsuccessful in its previous incarnation for one reason or another. Having explained in Chapter 9 why I believe there is no significant benefit in 'getting in at the start', I suggest that the date of first operation of a scheme is not a particularly useful piece of information, unless you have decided that you do *not* want to enter a brand-new scheme. Nevertheless, it has to be included.

2. The names and addresses of all of the promoters. This is a very important piece of information allowing you to follow up any queries you have about the scheme or the company. Only the very smallest of operations will be promoted by individuals or partnerships, as opposed to limited companies. In the case of a company the 'promoter' is, of course, the company itself.

3. A description of the goods or services which form the basis of the scheme. Hopefully, no one will join a scheme before finding out what products are involved – certainly not after reading this book anyway! Obviously, if you attend a meeting of any sort where an MLM business opportunity is being explained, you will find out what products are the subject of the business. However, on many types of promotional literature for MLM schemes distributed in the recent past there was no indication of what products were involved. The documents concentrated on the potential earnings of the concept itself. The reader will be well acquainted with the possibilities of MLM as a business method by now, and will realize that probably *the* most important aspect of an MLM scheme is the product(s). This requirement is particularly helpful, as many schemes are nothing but an abuse of the MLM concept, concerned mainly with transferring money from one person to another along with the pretence of selling a 'product', and sometimes without even that. Although many people are open-minded enough to examine a business opportunity without requiring specific details beforehand, I think it does no harm at all to make it clear to people what products are in fact involved.

4. A statement as to the capacity in which a participant will operate if he joins the scheme – whether he will be a servant or agent of the promoters, or one of the promoters, or whether he will act as a principal. If you intend to use documents of the kind mentioned above as a prospecting and recruitment tool, this information has to be in them.

5. A prominent and legible warning in the wording and format shown below, capital letters being at least 3mm high and the rectangular outline being at least 90mm by 30mm:

STATUTORY WARNING
1. Make sure that you understand what is being offered to you.
2. Do not be misled by claims that high earnings are easily achieved.
3. It is advisable to take independent legal advice before signing a contract.

Regulation 5   Lays down further requirements for the contents of documents of the kind mentioned above which are issued by MLM companies, when they contain any indications or suggestions that participants will derive a certain weekly, monthly or yearly income by joining the scheme. If this is done, then at the time when the document is issued the company must have evidence that those earnings have actually been obtained by one or more of the participants in the scheme, within the last three years. Directly underneath any such earnings statements, and equally as prominent, must be added the statement, 'The figures shown do not represent any automatic earnings. Actual earnings will depend on time and effort spent on the business and the total number of participants in the scheme.' (Attributing relevance to total number of participants in the scheme seems to suggest, wrongly, that 'saturation' is a practical rather than a theoretical problem. As no UK MLM scheme has ever had as many as 1 in 500 of the population as active distributors, sponsoring should not get more difficult at this level of participation. A scheme with a million distributors might begin to get more difficult to sponsor into, but this is quite unlikely to happen in the foreseeable future; *see* Chapter 9).

Regulation 6   Says that before any money is paid or agreed to be paid for goods or services which are to be supplied under the scheme, and before any goods or services are actually supplied to anyone under the scheme, the promoter and the participant shall have signed an agreement which contains all relevant terms of the scheme, and which complies with all the requirements of Regulation 7. The new participant must be given a copy of the agreement. This all seems pretty basic; after all, who in their right mind would start such a business without getting everything in writing beforehand? Unfortunately the answer is 'a lot of people'. Many of those who got their fingers burnt in some of the pyramid schemes found that when they needed to take up their grievances with the company, they had not a leg to stand on because there was no evidence of any agreement with the company.

Regulation 7   Lists information which must be included in the written agreements mentioned in Regulation 6.

1. The names and addresses of all of the promoters.
2. The date the scheme first came into operation in the UK (or the date of the proposed start of the operation).
3. A description of the goods or services which form the subject of the scheme.
4. An indication as to the capacity in which a participant will be acting if he joins the scheme, as servant or agent of the promoter or as a principal.
5. A legible and prominent warning in the wording and format shown below, the capital letters being at least 3mm high and the rectangular outline being at least 90mm by 30mm:

STATUTORY WARNING

Before you sign the contract:

(a) Make sure that you have read it carefully and that you have seen a document which explains the scheme in detail.

(b) Consider the following:

    1. It is advisable to take independent legal advice before signing a contract.

    2. Do not be misled by claims that high earnings are easily achieved.

    3. All businesses carry some risk. Do not purchase more stock then you believe you can sell in a reasonable period.

---

6. All the participants' rights in connection with termination of the contract, as described in Regulation 8 (see below).

Regulation 8 Lays down the participants' rights relating to terminating their distributorships. By reading through the list it will be apparent that each right conferred upon participants relates to a problem encountered with the pyramid schemes, which is now resolved by giving the distributors those rights. The rights are:

1. To terminate the distributorship at any time, without any penalty, by giving 14 days' written notice, starting from the day when the notice is posted first class.
2. Where such notice has been given within 14 days of the participant joining the scheme, a right to require the promoters

to repay any sums of money paid out in connection with the scheme, less any sum that may be owed for goods.

3. If notice of termination is given after 14 days, a right to require the promoters to buy back any goods purchased under the scheme at a price of at least 90 per cent of what the participant paid, unless the goods have deteriorated due to the participant's act or default. The refund is to be paid on delivery of the goods, or immediately if the promoter already holds them. The participant may also nominate a reasonable place to which he will deliver the goods within 21 days.

4. On termination, to be discharged from all contractual liabilities towards the promoters, except for those relating to payments made to the participant by customers under contracts which he made as an agent of the promoter, and of course except for the liability to pay for any goods which are not returned to the promoters.

5. If the promoter(s) decides to quit the scheme, a right to require him to give a full refund on any saleable goods returned by the participant. The refund is to be paid on delivery of the goods, or immediately if the promoter already holds them. The promoter may nominate a reasonable place of delivery, but must pay the cost of delivering the goods there.

Regulation 9 Restricts the amount of money which may be paid by a new participant within the first seven days of having joined a scheme. The 1973 regulations set this figure at £25, but from the 1 March 1990 it was raised to £75.

Regulation 10 Prohibits the taking of non-returnable deposits for goods supplied or to be supplied.

Regulation 11 Relaxes the previous requirement to make no charge for the provision of training facilities for participants, and allows chargeable training on condition that the cost has been clearly stated beforehand, and that it has been clearly explained to the participant that the use of the facility is not compulsory. If these requirements are not met, a participant is under no liability to pay for the facilities (Regulation 12).

Regulation 12 Explains the civil consequences of contraventions of these regulations:

1. Any payments accepted by a promoter or a participant in circumstances involving a contravention of Regulations 6, 9, 10 or 11, are recoverable by the participants who made them.
2. No agreement by a participant to make a payment is enforceable if there would be a contravention of Regulations 9, 10 or 11, or if the proper written agreement (Regulation 6) has not been made.
3. Companies should make very careful note of this paragraph, because if they supply goods to a participant in circumstances involving *any* contravention of the detailed requirements of Regulations 6, 7 and 8, the participant is under no liability to pay for the goods supplied. This seems to me to be a far stronger incentive to companies to make sure they follow the rules than the threat of prosecution!
4. As mentioned above, a participant cannot be required to pay for training facilities if Regulation 11 has not been followed.

Descriptions

Parts of the Trade Descriptions Act 1968 are worthy of study as they impinge upon almost every possible description that a company or a distributor may apply to every product, service or facility connected with a scheme.

The Act covers statements made 'in the course of a trade or business', which includes you, as there are not many circumstances where you could argue that participation in MLM was not in the course of a business. With regard to goods the Act simply says that it is an offence to apply a false description to them, or to supply them with a false description. You can be fairly sure that the products you will be dealing with will be packaged with a reasonable degree of care, and attention to legal requirements, at least if the company is at all worth your consideration. The products' labelling should leave nothing to be desired. You need to concern yourself with the descriptions that you (and your downline, as they will emulate you) make verbally to your customers or your prospects about the products. In other words, *don't exaggerate* the effectiveness, benefits, uses, performance or any other aspect of the products. In particular, if your business is in perfumes (an extremely popular MLM product), do not exaggerate their possible likenesses to those bearing famous names. This has so far been the area where most problems have occurred in relation to descriptions of MLM products. I have personally investigated complaints from customers of perfume distributors who had been given the firm impression that they were ordering a famous-name perfume, and who were understandably aggrieved to find that they received something that smelt only somewhat similar to it. These perfumes may smell like those you can buy in department stores for three times the price, and of course this is one of the reasons for their popularity, but they are *not* those perfumes, neither are they of exactly the same composition as those perfumes. Never mention other companies' names in connection with the goods that you are selling; in this way you can be sure that nobody ever gets the wrong impression about your goods.

It is extremely rare that an MLM company or distributor is actually prosecuted for such conduct, and in any case it would be very difficult to prove to the satisfaction of a court that an over-enthusiastic verbal false description was actually made. But it is not impossible. Don't be complacent in this respect because the most worrying effects of this type of conduct are the indirect consequences. If you go 'over the top' in your enthusiasm for the products you will find that your customers will soon realize the true facts about them and will avoid dealing with you in future. They may make complaints to Trading Standards offices which will be filed under your and the company's name. If your downline duplicate you this will compound the problem. If they don't, it means that they do not think your conduct is worth duplicating; either way is bad for your business, the company's business, and MLM in general.

Quoting membership of organizations is an area in which you should not be too vague or misleading, as a false statement could land you in trouble. The Direct Selling Association's membership, for instance, consists entirely of companies. An individual should not say that he is a member of the DSA even if the company with which he is associated *is* a member.

The Act also covers false statements about the provision or nature of any services or facilities which are made knowingly or recklessly. The opportunity to participate in an MLM scheme would appear to come within the meaning of 'facility', so you are therefore subject to the Act every time you explain your company's marketing plan. Make sure that you know exactly what you are talking about when you show the plan. People worth having in your business will go through the company's literature with a fine-tooth comb before signing anything, and they will soon discover any discrepancies between your story and the facts.

Prices

You need not have any problems at all with prices of the products you are selling. The company supplying them will give you all the information you will need for your customers about recommended prices, special offers, reductions and other discounts. You can assume that they will have done their homework and you are quite safe in quoting from the official literature. There may be instances, however, when you wish to develop your own promotions for goods, or compile your own advertisements which include prices. The following information is included for your reference in these cases.

The Consumer Protection Act 1987 prohibits misleading price indications in any form. Very simply, any price indications that you make (including verbal ones) should be clear, accurate and complete. If you are quoting a reduction from a previous price, you should state that previous price, make sure that it was your last price for those items, and make sure that it was available at that previous price for at least 28 consecutive days in the last six months. If you make an introductory offer, you should state the finishing date and keep to it. Only make comparisons with other manufacturers' products if:

- you are sure your information is accurate;
- you identify where those other products are being sold, and by whom;
- you refer to the same or substantially similar products.

You may only use a 'recommended price' if it is the price that your company recommends. You are not allowed to ascribe a 'worth' or 'value' to any products or services, even if someone else is selling the identical item for a higher price than you. If you charge for delivery or postage and packing you should show this clearly when you give the price of the goods. It should go without saying that VAT must always be included in your prices.

The above-mentioned requirements are only the most relevant ones which may apply to an MLM distributor. For full details of how to comply with the Consumer Protection Act with regard to pricing, contact the Department of Trade and Industry for their booklet, *Code of Practice for Traders on Price Indications*. It might also be available from Trading Standards offices.

Cancellation

In 1987, primarily to protect purchasers of expensive home improvement products sold to them on their own premises by pushy salespeople, regulations were made giving cancellation rights to consumers in certain transactions. Any contract worth £35 or more which is signed away from the business premises of the seller can be cancelled without penalty within seven days from the making of the contract. Additionally, all such purchasers must be given written notice of their rights in this regard when they sign the contract. Although it may not be a very common occurrence to deliver orders over £35 to your customers, when you do you must make sure that these requirements are followed. No doubt your MLM company will supply you with all the necessary paperwork. For reference, the regulations are called the Consumer Protection (cancellation of contracts concluded away from business premises) Regulations 1987.

Copyright

The rules of copyright are contained in the Copyright, Designs and Patents Act 1988. Copyright does not have to be applied for, registered or paid for. It subsists in every original musical, dramatic, literary and artistic work. It belongs to the author of the work (or the person who commissioned it) and gives exclusive rights to that person to control the making and distributing of further copies of that work. The Act gives extensive powers to copyright owners to protect their work, including the power to seize infringing copies in some circumstances, and also provides that offences are committed by persons dealing in infringing copies in the course of business.

In MLM, it is not uncommon to find that distributors, in their enthusiasm to build their business, resort to many types of copying activities in order to supplement their literature and sales and business aids. Usually these activities are carried out on a very small scale, and in any case the author would have an impossible task enforcing his rights. For example, have you ever unlawfully copied music from a compact disc on to a tape? We have all done this, and we all know that we are not going to be sued by the record companies for doing it because it would be impossible for them to do so in every case of home recording. Other copyright infringements, however, can have more serious effects. Take, for instance, the case of a promotional video tape issued by an MLM company to assist in sponsoring. It will probably have professional actors and other people featured, most of whom will have agreed with your company a fee and/or a royalty percentage, just as the company has agreed to pay *you* a royalty on sales by your organization. Unauthorized copying of the video will prevent the payment of legitimate royalties due to the actors and other people involved in its production. How would you feel about somebody depriving you of the legitimate royalties due from your business? The same arguments apply to audio tapes, magazine articles, book extracts, and so on. There should be no doubt about what can and cannot be copied as the work itself will normally bear a warning statement to that effect. If you are in any doubt, contact the company, or the author of the work.

Trade marks

Closely related to the concept of copyright, a trade mark is usually a design or unique set of words which is applied to a commodity to identify the manufacturer. A trade mark may be registered, in which case it is then protected by law against unauthorized use. A trade mark can consist merely of a few letters forming one or two words which are then applied to certain products. The words may be ones that are used in everyday speech, but when they are applied to the relevant products they become trade marks. MLM distributors selling perfumes again need to be extremely careful in making comparisons. The advice given above in connection with trade descriptions will stand you in good stead as far as trade marks are concerned.

Most MLM companies will have created their own products and given them names which they will have registered as trade marks. Companies do this to give their products an identity, a good reputation synonymous with the reputation of the company. They are understandably very fussy about how their marks are used, and in many cases will have strict rules covering distributors' use of them. If you want to have a harmonious relationship with your company, read their terms and conditions carefully.

Advertising

Due to the nature of the MLM business, advertising of products by the companies rarely takes place. There is much advertising by distributors, though, for products or recruits or both; pick up any local newspaper and turn to the 'situations vacant' and 'part-time vacancies' columns to see evidence of this. All of the above paragraphs apply to advertisements, and so do a number of other rules and regulations, as detailed below. Make sure you are well acquainted with what you should and shouldn't do in any advertising.

If all your advertisements are legal, decent, honest and truthful you should not go too far wrong. These four adjectives are the cornerstone of the Advertising Standards Authority's Code of Advertising Practice. The code can be obtained from the ASA or from your local Trading Standards office, and contains detailed requirements to which all advertisers have to adhere. Complaints to the ASA by anyone aggrieved or upset by an advertisement are investigated and, if upheld, the advertiser is asked to make an assurance that there will be no repeat of the advertisement. If an assurance is not given, or not followed, the ASA can instruct all advertising media to refuse to accept further advertisements from the offending advertiser. As a specific example, the ASA upheld a complaint from a member of the public who answered an advertisement stating '10 overweight people wanted to try a new weight control programme', or words to that effect. The complainant said that she thought she was volunteering for some kind of research, and did not expect to be approached instead to buy diet products from a distributor. The advertisement was plainly dishonest.

The ASA has also in the past upheld complaints regarding recruitment advertisements which were placed in 'situations vacant' columns in such a way as to lead people to think that paid employment was being offered. The advertiser in this case might have been hoping that someone looking for employment might also be interested in a business of their own. It is wrong to mislead people like this, because they can waste time and money finding out about something which never interested them in the first place. If you want to advertise for distributors, make sure that you place the advertisement in a 'business opportunities' column if one is available. Otherwise, make it perfectly clear that you are offering a business opportunity and not a job.

Remember that when you advertise you will be acting 'in the course of a trade or business', however small your business might be at that time. The Business Advertisements (Disclosure) Order requires that your advertisements make clear that fact. Some newspapers suggest a 'T' at the end of your wording or you can make the situation clear by using a business name, like 'Joan's Health and Beauty Supplies'. Alternatively, if your advertisement reads something like 'We can supply all types of environmentally-friendly laundry and cleaning products . . .', it is clear enough that you are in a business.

You will perhaps be able to offer through your business some high-cost items for which the company offers credit facilities. They will be able to do this because they are licenced under the Consumer Credit Act to do so. *You* are almost certainly not licenced, and therefore you must not make any reference to credit in your advertisements. You become a credit broker if you do so, for which you need a licence, and there are strict requirements governing advertisements offering credit.

Finally, the rules of conduct by which you agree to abide when you sign up with a company are certain to include matters relating to advertising of the company's products, or at the very least a general statement with regard to the manner in which distributors are expected to conduct their business. It is as well to be familiar with these rules as it will avoid any problems or misunderstandings with your company.

Ethics

This covers the moral aspects of the way a business is run. It is entirely up to you whether your business is run on highly ethical principles, but I do believe that in the long run you will be more successful if you do things 'right'. Here are some of the activities which will leave a bad taste, and perhaps discredit your business and MLM generally.

An invitation to see a presentation of the business opportunity should be quite clear as to exactly what it is. People get very put out when they attend what they think is some kind of social event and find that it is nothing of the sort, especially if they are put under any kind of pressure to buy products or sign up into a business. This type of deceptive invitation has been the source of many official complaints in the past; hopefully in the past is where they will stay.

Another activity of rather too enthusiastic distributors has been the accosting of people in the street (true!). One mild-mannered young man I know was put quite ill at ease and almost frightened by being approached in the street by a talkative extrovert who started up a conversation with him by remarking, 'That's a terrific jacket you're wearing, where did you get it?' Within one minute he was asking, 'Would you like to know how to make a lot of money?' There is nothing intrinsically wrong with this, but it puts people off and invariably gives them the impression that all MLM people are the same.

The service offered by British Telecom, whereby they sell 0898 numbers connected to answering machines which give 'information' from the subscriber, has been abused more often than not. The caller pays up to 38 pence per minute to listen to the message on the tape, and the subscriber retains a large chunk of that amount. There are some excellent information services offered on 0898 numbers, notably medical advisory services, but the most common use is for aural sex, advertised in the most popular daily tabloids. The most objectionable use of the 0898 numbers, however, is for giving out straightforward simple information, like an address or another telephone number, in the most long-winded way possible when that information could easily have been included in the advertisement. This is how some MLM distributors try to supplement their income when advertising for recruits. There is an attractive advertisement offering easy money, a five-, six- or seven-minute message (£2 or more for every call), ending with the distributor's name or telephone number. It is despicable, and against some MLM companies' rules of conduct.

Most MLM companies give excellent guarantees on their products and they rightly expect you to honour them. What tends to happen, of course, is that you will have put forth superhuman efforts in one month and just managed to scrape into a higher level on the 30th of the month. Then along will come Mrs Smith with her three bottles of perfume, saying, 'It just doesn't smell like I remember it smelling at the party. Can I have a refund?' Despite your expected bonus cheque shrinking before your eyes because you won't reach the higher level after all, you should give your nicest smile and say, 'Of course you can Mrs Smith. As I told you at the party, our guarantees are unconditional!' Not everyone can bring themselves to act in this way, though. One complaint was made about a perfume distributor who decided that her business was not going to be spoilt by awkward customers, however much fuss they made. I imagine that her business is still rather small, if it still exists. Honour all guarantees . . . with a smile!

Never denigrate competitors' products. It is a small-minded, unprofessional thing to do. You probably do not know enough about the other product to give an authoritative view on it, anyway. It will appear to your customer that, in order to give your product some credibility, you have to run down the other one. If you manage to get your facts wrong about the other product and your customer is aware of this, your credibility immediately hits rock bottom. Besides, the customer might have used that other product before and thought it was very good, in which case you will have a hard job convincing him to buy yours. The big thinker will always praise the competition and will come over as confident and assured of the quality of his product. He will be much more likely to sell his product.

What about delivering leaflets door to door warning people that their health is in danger unless they start using your products? This has happened with water filtration systems, and for good measure the business name of the distributor and the wording of the leaflet led recipients to believe that the communication was from the water authority. This particular leaflet then informed the householder that a representative would call the following day (like it or not) to carry out a test which would prove how polluted the drinking water was. Can you imagine the effect of this campaign on old and vulnerable people? The water authority received many calls from worried householders that week. This type of sales campaign brings direct selling itself into disrepute. You wouldn't even *think* of doing business in this manner, would you?

MLM companies do not like other companies' distributors poaching theirs, and who can blame them? There are millions of people all around you who have never heard of MLM and who might be looking for something just like it. The evidence available indicates that most of the successful MLM distributors joined their company's scheme at a time when they knew nothing of MLM. If you still feel that you must approach current distributors, there are right and wrong ways of doing it. The wrong way is to creep around the car park of a concert hall where an MLM company is having its annual convention and put advertisements for your company under the windscreen wipers of all the distributors' cars. A 'right way' (if there is one) is to advertise generally and follow up each enquirer, but it is unethical to approach directly other companies' distributors or distributors from other groups in your own company's organization.

The Direct Selling Association

Many MLM companies are members of the DSA (ten at the time of writing), and to be admitted they have to agree to abide by the DSA Code of Practice. This code binds the companies *and* their distributors, so you should make yourself aware of its requirements and stick to its principles at all times. The use of the DSA logo by a company or an individual gives a message – a trade description – to all who see it that the DSA rules are followed by them. Failure to follow the rules will not only jeopardize the membership of the company, but may render them, and possibly you, liable to prosecution for giving a false trade description. The Code of Practice is available from any member company or the DSA, whose address is 44 Russell Square, London WC1B 4JP (telephone: 071 580 8433). For quick reference, the main rules pertaining to the conduct of distributors are as follows (the numbers quoted refer to the paragraphs of the Code):

2 Party and business presentation invitations must be perfectly clear as to what the purpose of the occasion is.

3 Sales persons shall act with integrity. Their sales presentations must be truthful and they must respect a customer's request to refuse further discussion. The Office of Fair Trading's guidelines on telephone selling shall be followed.

6 Sales people should immediately identify themselves to prospective customers, and indicate the purpose of their approach, the products they deal in, and the company with which they are associated.

7 Customers are to be given the name and address of the company and indicate that they are DSA members. A copy of the Code of Practice should be available for perusal.

10 Customers must be made aware of their right to cancel any order within fourteen days of making it.

Afterword

Now you know all about multi-level marketing. You know what it is, what it can do for you financially and otherwise, how it works, how to make it work for you, how others have made it work for them, how to do it properly and how to decide who to do it with. If you have read and digested all of the information within this book you will know more about the subject than 99 per cent of the people who are involved in the business, and 100 per cent of those who are not.

If you do not yet have an MLM business and were interested enough in the subject to read all about it you now have no excuse not to start immediately. If you already have an MLM business you now have no excuse not to make it as successful as you really want it to be. Either way, there's nothing to lose and everything to gain.

They say there are only three types of people:

- those who make things happen;
- those who watch things happen; and
- those who say 'what happened?'

In which category are you?

Appendix 1

Multi-level marketing companies in the UK

I am apprehensive about presenting a list of currently operating MLM companies which could well be out of date by the time you read it, but nowhere else can a prospective participant find anything approaching such a listing. It would be wrong to introduce you to the fantastic possibilities of MLM through this book and then leave you to find out for yourself what schemes are available; you might well not find out about the one which would be ideal for you. Obviously, any member company of the DSA offers a worthwhile and thoroughly vetted opportunity, but prospective members and non-member companies may also offer perfectly good schemes.

In the following pages, therefore, there is a reasonably comprehensive list of companies which are at the time of writing operating in the UK offering a multi-level marketing business opportunity. I make no claims, comments or recommendations at all about any aspect of these companies, their products or their opportunities. If you are not already involved in MLM and you have decided that it is the business for you, study the list, make an initial assessment as to which one or more companies might appeal to you, get hold of the full facts from the companies (you will probably be referred to a nearby distributor), and, with the help of the advice given in Chapter 4, make your decision. The list will be updated in future editions of this book.

AMWAY (UK) LTD (DSA member)
Snowdon Drive
Winterhill
Milton Keynes
MK6 1AR
0908 679888

Household cleaning and laundry products, kitchenware, cookware and plasticware items. Car care products. Cosmetics. Perfumes. Personal care items. Vitamin supplements and diet foods. Fitness equipment. Financial services. SKY satellite TV package. Portable telephones.

BEE NATURAL PRODUCTS (UK) LTD
Goodnestone Road
Wingham
Kent
CT3 1AR
0227 720881

Skin care products and food supplements based on Royal Jelly.

CAMBRIDGE NUTRITION LTD
69–75 Thorpe Road
Norwich
NR1 1HY
0603 760777

Diet foods and drinks.

CHRISTIAN CHABRIS LTD
102 Garratt Lane
London SW18 4DJ
081 874 6400

Perfumes and jewellery.

FOREVER LIVING PRODUCTS (UK) LTD
35 Piccadilly
London
W1V 9PB
071 439 8985

Nutritional supplements. Skin and personal care products.

FRENCH COLLECTION (UK) LTD
Unit 7
Airfield Road
Ambassador Estate
Christchurch
Dorset
0202 490102

Cosmetics and skin care products.

FRENCH OPTIONS LTD
'Byfield'
Green Walk
Bowden
Altrincham
Cheshire
WA14 2TQ
061 927 7343

Perfumes and accessories.

HERBALIFE (UK) LTD (DSA member)
Unit 6/7
Perth Trading Estate
Perth Ave
Slough
SL1 4XY
0753 77711

Diet foods. Vitamin and herbal supplements. Hair and skin care products. Water treatment system.

JANNE LTD
High Billinge House
Quarry Bank
Utkinton
Tarporley
Cheshire
CW6 0LA
0829 8644

Jewellery.

KLEENEZE HOMECARE LTD (DSA member)
Martins Road
Hanham
Bristol
BS15 3DY
0272 670861

Large range of household cleaning and laundry products. Brushes of all descriptions. Kitchen plasticware and other household goods. Car care products.

L'AROME (UK) LTD (DSA member)
Parkway
Deeside Industrial Park
Deeside
Clwyd CH5 2NS
0244 830383

Perfumes and accessories.

LIFEVISION INTERNATIONAL LTD
102 Garratt Lane
London
SW18 4DJ
081 874 6446

Herbal nutritional drink. Skin care products.

L R INTERNATIONAL (UK) LTD
Racine House
Plum Lane
Dunwear
Bridgwater
Somerset
TA6 5HL
0278 455550

Perfumes, cosmetics, skin care products.

MUSIC WORLD
Warwick House
12 Warwick Road
Wordsley
West Midlands
DY8 5DL
0964 543956

Records, compact discs, audio and video tapes (pre-recorded and blank). Various accessories.

NATIONAL SAFETY ASSOCIATES OF AMERICA (UK) LTD
(DSA member)
NSA House
39 Queen Street
Maidenhead
Berkshire SL6 1NB
0628 776044

Water treatment systems.

NATURE'S SUNSHINE PRODUCTS INC. (DSA member)
Unit 5
Hortonwood 32
Telford
Shropshire
TF1 4EX
0952 670151

Vitamin, mineral and herbal supplements. Skin care products. Diet products. Herbal beverages. Water treatment systems.

NON-SCENTS INC.
40 Upper Richmond Road
Putney
London
SW15 2TX
081 874 3323

Natural mineral odour removal product.

NUTRI-METICS INTERNATIONAL (UK) (DSA member)
Erica Road
Stacey Bushes
Milton Keynes
MK12 6HS
0908 262020

Skin care and cosmetics.

OUR SECRET COLLECTION LTD (DSA member)
67 Victoria Road
Burgess Hill
Sussex
H15 9LH
0444 870550

Perfumes. Jewellery. Skin care products.

POWERPLUS CLEANBURN LTD
143 Millbrook Road East
Southampton
SO1 0HQ
0703 232929

Vehicle fuel modification unit.

**RICHWAY INTERNATIONAL PRODUCTS
CORPORATION LTD**
Unit 8
54 Kings Hill
Beech
Alton
Hampshire
GU3 4AN

Herbal food supplements and bodycare products. Water purifier.

THE HAIR COMPANY
82–90 Kelvin Avenue
Hillington
Glasgow
G52
041 882 8300

Hair and personal care items. Aromatherapy products. Perfumes.

UNI-VITE LTD (DSA member)
50 Aylesbury Road
Aston Clinton
Aylesbury
Buckinghamshire
HP22 5AH
0296 631177

Diet foods and drinks. Some food supplements and skin care products.

Appendix 2

Fundraising

A particularly useful benefit of the MLM system is its potential application as a fast and effective method of raising funds for clubs and charities, while at the same time profiting its members and supporters. The organization itself, or perhaps a nominated member of its committee, is sponsored into a suitable MLM company, ideally by a sponsor who is sympathetic to the cause. The company chosen should be solid and well established and, most importantly, its products must appeal to the majority of the charity's supporters or the club's members. Some expense has to be incurred initially in the production of suitable literature explaining the concept and its benefits to the organization and everyone involved. This is an area where the sponsors may wish to assist, bearing in mind that they will ultimately benefit from the venture.

There are many ways in which the idea can be put into practice, but perhaps the most effective way is to set a reasonably achievable target for each participant – to purchase a small amount of product each month (for personal use or resale), and to sponsor three or five others who will agree to do the same for a good cause. It is important that each participant makes a commitment to reaching the target set by the committee. The club or charity should initially sponsor enough people to ensure a reasonable wholesale and royalty income when the project takes off, probably a minimum of five. The organization can be content with the income generated to it from the project, or it may also decide to require each participant to donate a certain amount of their profits from the enterprise.

Because of the charitable aspect of the operation, the members may find it easier to recruit people and sell products than they would normally. The added bonus, of course, in such a novel method of fundraising, is that the fundraisers themselves make a profit by helping their organization. This may even inspire them to seriously work the business for their own benefit, which will assist the organization even more.

I should stress again the importance of choosing the right product or products. Unless they are of good quality and value (preferably consumable, giving repeat sales), with the potential for popularity with the type of people sympathetic to the aims of the organization, it may become a struggle to maintain enthusiasm for the campaign beyond the first month or two.

I should also add that many companies have ongoing charitable fundraising activities in operation as a regular feature, payments being made direct from the companies from sales profits. Ultimately, through MLM fundraising, more charities may benefit than originally intended!

Appendix 3

Further reading

Allen, James E (1985) *As a Man Thinketh*, Brownlow Publishers, Fort Worth.

Bettger, Frank (1989) *How I Raised Myself from Failure to Success in Selling*, Cedar Books, London.

Carnegie, Dale (1986) *How to Win Friends and Influence People*, Cedar Books, London.

Danforth, William (1931) *I Dare You*, I Dare You, Saint Louis.

Hill, Napoleon (1983) *Think and Grow Rich*, Fawcett (Division of Ballantine Books).

Hill, Napoleon, and Stone, W Clement (1987) *Success through a Positive Mental Attitude*, Pocket Books, Simon and Schuster, New York.

Holland, Ron (1989) *Talk and Grow Rich*, Thorsons Publishers Ltd, Wellingborough, Northants.

Maltz, Maxwell (1980) *Psycho Cybernetics*, Thorsons Publishers Ltd, Wellingborough, Northants.

Mandino, Og (1987) *The Greatest Salesman in the World*, Bantam Books, New York.

Mandino, Og (1983) *The Greatest Secret in the World*, Bantam Books, New York.

Roller, David (1989) *How to Make Big Money in Multi-Level Marketing*, Prentice-Hall, Inc.

Schwartz, David (1984) *The Magic of Getting What you Want*, Berkley, New York.

Schwartz, David (1984) *The Magic of Thinking Big*, Thorsons Publishers Ltd, Wellingborough, Northants.

Sweetland, Ben (1976) *I can*, Wilshire Book Co., North Hollywood.

Sweetland, Ben *I will*, Wilshire Book Co., North Hollywood.

Vincent Peale, Norman (1986) *The Power of Positive Thinking*, Cedar Books, London.

Waitley, Dennis (1988) *Seeds of Greatness*, Pocket Books, Simon and Schuster, New York.

Waitley, Dennis (1988) *The Psychology of Winning*, Nightingale Conant, Chicago.

Sources of information

Direct Selling Association
44 Russell Square
London
WC1B 4JP

An association of direct selling companies, one-third of which use MLM structures.

Multi-level Marketing, International Association
Capital House
6 Quay Haven
Swanwick
Southampton
SO3 7DE

An association of MLM companies, distributors and support groups, whose stated objective is 'to set and maintain new levels of honesty, integrity and professionalism throughout the MLM industry'.

Direct Sales Agents' Association
1 Bell Tower Industrial Estate
Roedean Road
Brighton
East Sussex
BN2 5RU

An association of independent business people in direct sales with the aim of creating 'a body strong enough to represent its members' interests in all situations where individual action might be inadequate'.

Department of Trade and Industry (Consumer Affairs Division 3)
10–18 Victoria Street
London
SW1H 0NN

The government department responsible for the production, promulgation and enforcement of legislation relating to MLM.

Market Link
Marsden
The Strand
Starcross
Exeter
EX6 8PA

Publisher of useful guides: *The Independent Operator's Guide to MLM* and *The Lucky 21*.

Any further enquiries can be addressed to:

Peter J. Clothier
c/o Kogan Page Ltd
120 Pentonville Road
London N1 9JN

Index